I Sing the Salmon Home

This book is made possible in part by the Academy of American Poets Laureate Fellowship Program with funds from the Mellon Foundation.

academy of american poets

The editor and publisher also thank the following organizations for their support of this project.

WASHINGTON STATE
ARTS COMMISSION

I Sing the Salmon Home

Poems from Washington State

Edited by Rena Priest

Empty Bowl Press
Chimacum, Washington

Empty Bowl Press, founded in 1976 as a cooperative letterpress publisher, has produced periodicals, broadsides, literary anthologies, collections of poetry, fiction, essays, and books of Chinese translations. Our mission is to publish the work of writers who share Empty Bowl's founding purpose, "literature and responsibility," and its fundamental theme, the love and preservation of human communities in wild places.

ISBN 978-1-7370408-9-7
Library of Congress Control Number: 2023930785

Cover art: Joseph (wahalatsuʔ) Seymour Jr. (Squaxin Island/Pueblo of Acoma), *The Run That Used to Be,* 2022. Acrylic on paper, 3'×3'
Interior art: Jason LeClair, *Salmon Egg*
Cover design: Lauren Grosskopf

A portion of the sales from this collection will be donated to the Save Our wild Salmon coalition in support of their efforts to restore abundant wild salmon populations in the Pacific Northwest. Save Our wild Salmon is a diverse, nationwide coalition working to protect and restore wild salmon and steelhead to the rivers, streams, and marine waters of the Pacific Northwest for the benefit of our region's ecology, economy, and cultures. www.wildsalmon.org.

Empty Bowl Press
www.emptybowl.org
editor@emptybowl.org

I don't believe in magic. I believe in the sun and the stars, the water, the tides, the floods, the owls, the hawks flying, the river running, the wind talking. They're measurements. They tell us how healthy things are. How healthy we are. Because we and they are the same. That's what I believe in. Those who learn to listen to the world that sustains them can hear the message brought forth by salmon.

Billy Frank Jr.

Contents

Wild, Sacred

Sojourn

Invisible Thread

Fish School

Gratitude

Choices

Vigil

What We Owe

Preface

Ey' Skweyel Ne'schaleche! I'm so happy this book has found its way into your hands. Its journey from the minds of poets onto these pages has been nothing short of heroic. Perhaps not quite as heroic as the journey of a salmon, but drawing inspiration from it.

I was recently asked during an interview what gave me the idea for the anthology, and I remarked that I'd read these words from Billy Frank Jr. in Timothy Egan's book *The Good Rain:* "The golden egg of the Northwest was this guy, the salmon, and they were destroying the golden egg. . . . It's taken more than a hundred years. But I tell my people to get ready. Get your smokehouses back in shape. Don't forget the ceremonies. That guy, the salmon, he's coming back."

I liked the way Billy Frank Jr. called the salmon "that guy." It was so affectionate and familiar, and in keeping with how I think of them—scrappy, formidable, and generous. Frank's talk of that guy inspired me and filled me with a feeling of hopeful possibility that there's still time for the wild salmon runs of the Pacific Northwest. I wanted to do something to celebrate salmon through poetry and to offer gratitude for all that they contribute to the bounty and beauty of this place we love and call home.

This is all true, but thinking back even further, I recall a conversation I had with Bellingham poet Andrew Shattuck McBride in the lobby of the Pickford Film Center in 2018. At that time, he was coediting the anthology *For Love of Orcas* with Orcas Island poet Jill McCabe Johnson, and he asked if I'd be interested in jumping in as another coeditor on the project.

Unfortunately, I was overwhelmed with a lot of other work, so I had to decline. He asked what my dream project would be, and I told him that I'd really like to someday collect poems for a salmon anthology, because while orcas are an indicator species—meaning they tell us how well we're doing overall (not that great)—salmon are a keystone species, which means everything relies on them, and if we want to be okay, the salmon must thrive.

With the magic that happens when you voice a wish to the universe, four years later, here we are. This is the dream anthology, and as if by fate, the most fitting title for the anthology comes from McBride's poem "Winter Run, Whatcom Creek," in which he writes, "I sing the salmon home" and "I cheer the salmon on." Assembling this book has truly been a wonderful journey for me. Everything has moved along with the feeling that the spirit of the salmon is cheering me on, helping me bring this book into the world.

When things are meant to be, things fortuitously fall into place and a path is made clear. Working on a collaboration grant from the National Geographic Society helped me understand the urgency of saving our wild salmon runs. Appointment as Washington State Poet Laureate meant that I had the support of Humanities Washington and the Washington State Arts Commission, which gave me the platform and reach to assemble work from poets across the state.

An Academy of American Poets Laureate Fellowship provided the means to produce the anthology, and a partnership with Empty Bowl Press meant that the publishing expertise of Holly J. Hughes and John Pierce were in play. The Washington State Center for the Book and Washington State Librarian will provide homes and access to more than 350 copies of the collection, and, of course, most important, Washington State poets have shared their beautiful poetry and goodwill toward our wild Washington salmon runs.

After the official announcement of the Laureate Fellowship was made by the Academy of American Poets in August 2022, I put out an open call across the state. Submissions closed on October 1, and in those few short months, we received more than five hundred poems from over three hundred poets. Then the hard work of making selections began. This was the most difficult phase of the process.

So many wonderful works were submitted. It was hard to choose which would be collected. After painstaking deliberation, I delivered a table of contents to Empty Bowl Press on December 1, 2022. It has been a beautiful adventure, to which I am honored to have been called.

In keeping with the generosity of poets and wild salmon, proceeds from this anthology will go to support operational costs of Empty Bowl Press and a donation will be made to Save Our wild Salmon so that poets and salmon can continue their important work of nourishing our spirits and bodies.

The life cycle of this anthology as I've outlined above is only part of that story, for I am a Lhaq'temish woman—a member of the Lummi Nation. We are salmon people. Lummi is a fishing culture. We invented the reef net—an innovative technology dating back more than ten thousand years.

The reef net relies on community inclusion and participation. Two canoes anchor side by side, and the net is set in the water between them. A false reef is created to lure salmon upward and to the net. When the salmon run between the canoes, the reef-net captain shouts, and the crew lifts the net, hauling in their catch. In the cosmology of the reef net, the net symbolizes a womb, and the salmon are the sacred spark of life that will carry the people into another cycle.

Prior to colonization, nets were woven by family matriarchs who contributed a panel of net to be stitched together with the panels made by other matriarchs. This community effort created a bond between the families; a matriarch's contribution ensured her family a share of the catch. Doesn't that sound beautiful?

It is my hope that the poems in this collection will carry into the hearts of readers a wish to preserve and protect the gifts of salmon bestowed by a beautiful living earth; that they will provide the spark of life to carry us into a new cycle. It is my hope that stitching together these poems will bond the poets in real life as well as in these pages—that they may find and acknowledge each other in community, now and ever after.

I was told that when we are called to sacred work we can't say no, and we can never turn our back on it. The poets in these pages have answered the call and now are forever bound to it. They speak to the heroism of the salmon's journey. They rail against the dams and pollution that interrupt that blessed epic. They whisper hope, and they console with gratitude. May their good work continue to sing the salmon home.

Yohamest,
Rena Priest
Ce'Whel'tenaut
Washington State Poet Laureate, 2021–2023

Introduction

Our simplest wisdom is to follow the sea-bright salmon home.

Tom Jay, "The Salmon of the Heart"

In a favorite snapshot of me as a kid, I'm holding up the first fish I caught. The photo was taken in Minnesota—the fish was a sunfish, and a small one at that. But there's no mistaking the glint of pride in my eyes, reflecting what I knew instinctively in my six-year-old bones: fish would be my teacher in the decades to come.

Twenty years later, another snapshot: I'm wearing yellow raingear over a grimy, red-hooded sweatshirt and a blue baseball cap. In my arms, I'm cradling a sleek silver king salmon, minutes from the sea. That same glint of pride is in my eyes, though the emotion is more complicated. I've found myself fishing for a living, gillnetting for salmon in Southeast Alaska. From the first salmon we caught, which we ceremonially released, to the last, it was never easy for me to kill a creature as beautiful as a salmon, especially one on such an extraordinary journey. I confess that during those years, I let many salmon swim free. After eight years, I left fishing, but those years gave me an intimate relationship with salmon—a hands-on appreciation for their beauty, strength, and courage—and a teacher I still turn to for guidance and inspiration.

Given my history with salmon as a student, reluctant catcher, and grateful receiver, I'm honored to be invited to write the introduction to *I Sing the Salmon Home.* Three decades after I left fishing, it feels fitting to circle back to those endless summer days at sea following the salmon runs north. Even more fitting, it turns out that *introduction* means to be led into the circle.

A circle is an apt image for writing about salmon, who leave the stream of their birth in an epic journey to circumnavigate the Pacific Ocean, eventually finding their way back to their native stream. Days later, after the female deposits her eggs in the redd and the male swims alongside to fertilize them, they die and drift downstream, becoming food for eagle, bear, and raven, decomposing along the stream, their seagoing nutrients absorbed by the roots of the cedar trees, completing a critical ecological circle.

Freeman House, in his classic collection of essays *Totem Salmon: Life Lessons from Another Species,* elaborates on the role of salmon as teacher:

> Salmon, who spend most of their lives hidden from us in the vast oceans, return to us to instruct us and feed us. They focus our attention on some of the smaller increments of our natural world—the streams that run through

our rural homes or beneath our urban structures—at the same time as they instruct us regarding the indivisible relationship of one locale to another and the life lessons to be learned from other species.

While biologists may only recently be documenting these ecological connections, for Indigenous people this knowledge is centuries old. For tribes in the Northwest, salmon are not merely food. Extending all the way up the coast to Alaska, the Indigenous tribes who live on the Northwest coast proudly consider themselves Salmon People. Their identity, seasonal rhythms, and ceremonies revolve around the return of the salmon each fall and drying fish for the winter ahead. Salmon are welcomed into their lives—most tribes celebrate the return of the first salmon—and honored in their ceremonies and art. Their relationship with salmon is one of reciprocity, and they treat the salmon accordingly, with reverence and respect.

When Lewis and Clark reached the Northwest in the early 1800s, the salmon runs were so plentiful, they wrote in their field journals, "you could walk across the rivers on their silvery backs." Flash forward two centuries, and those legendary salmon runs are depleted to the point that many runs are extinct and the rest endangered. Today the hydroelectric dams on the Snake and Columbia Rivers that have provided cheap electricity for decades have exacted their price. Combine that with pollution and habitat destruction as the region has grown and more recent threats posed by climate change—warmer streams for spawning resulting in lower oxygen levels as well as other changes to ocean chemistry that we're just beginning to understand. And as we're becoming acutely aware, the fate of the local orca populations is inextricably tied to dwindling Chinook runs, dependent as the resident orcas are on abundant quantities of the fat-laden salmon.

There's small consolation in learning that we're not the first region to lose our salmon runs; this pattern has been repeated around the world, according to David Montgomery, author of *King of Fish: The Thousand Year Run of Salmon.* In his book, Montgomery chronicles the loss of salmon runs globally, beginning with native runs in England and Europe in the nineteenth century and continuing on the eastern seaboard in North America until he reaches the Pacific Northwest, where wild salmon still return to streams in Washington, British Columbia, and Alaska.

Montgomery points out a common theme in the demise of salmon runs: a chasm between what people want and what politicians are willing to do—and how long that takes. As he explains, political wheels take time to turn and salmon can't afford to wait: "What we're facing now requires not just our best science and technology but more: a creative response," he wrote twenty years ago, in 2003. "Today, our solutions are not just stream restoration but may require breaching the dams."

Thankfully, there's precedent. After the Elwha River dam was breached on September 17, 2011, the Elwha River salmon knew exactly what to do. When the salmon returned, they headed up the river and spawned, exceeding fisheries biologists' predictions in their numbers despite having been cut off from those spawning grounds for generations.

Meanwhile, voices calling for breaching the four dams on the lower Snake River have grown louder, with the tribes who live along the Columbia River the most insistent. In the last few years, legislation proposing to breach those dams is gaining bipartisan support, although it still faces resistance from industries in the region dependent on cheap hydropower. As this collection goes to press, we're at a hinge moment, with salmon providing an opportunity for us to come together to protect them from extinction.

Years ago, this sentiment was voiced by one of the Northwest's most passionate advocates for salmon, Nisqually tribal member Billy Frank Jr., when he said, "If the salmon could speak, he would ask us to help him survive. This is something we must tackle together." Billy Frank modeled this sentiment in his many years as chairman of the Northwest Indian Fisheries Commission, working effectively with native leaders and nonnative politicans alike in response to the landmark Boldt Decision (named after United States District Court Judge George H. Boldt) in 1975, which upheld treaty rights by allocating 50 percent of the harvestable salmon return to twenty local tribes. In honor of Billy Frank's lifelong dedication to fighting for treaty rights and protecting the salmon runs, we've included his wise words as an epigraph for this collection.

More wise words were spoken by Ursula K. Le Guin upon receiving the Lifetime Achievement award at the National Book Awards in 2014: "Any human power can be resisted and changed by human beings. Resistance and change often begin in art." In that spirit, Washington State Poet Laureate Rena Priest has assembled this anthology. From the more than five hundred poems that were submitted, she's brought together poems that speak to the power of our collective relationship with salmon. In *I Sing the Salmon Home,* the poems take many forms and reflect many voices: you'll find haiku, villanelles, and pantoums; you'll find poems written by kids, elders, sport fishers, commercial fishers, biologists, and citizens of local tribal nations. You'll find poems that express awe and gratitude, and you'll find poems that express grief and anger at a worldview that pursues profit at the expense of the salmon, all joining together here to sing the salmon home.

Weaving through all these poems is the indomitable spirit of the salmon heading upstream against all odds. May we learn from our teacher. May we complete the circle. May we make the hard choices needed to ensure that they survive and thrive. May the words so beautifully gathered here sing the salmon home for centuries to come.

Holly J. Hughes
Copublisher
Empty Bowl Press

I Sing the Salmon Home

Wild, Sacred

I Went Looking for the Wild One

I went looking for the wild one, the howler, the vatic
tramp, the one for whom the wounded hillsides
are inner burns, whose blood is stained
with the old love-wine of poet and earth—
warrior poet, slinging battle flak out at the static,
shattering polite conversations everywhere.

I looked in the anthologies, listening for echoes, traced for
signs in the quarterlies, magazines, best-ofs. I learned it's
been a good year for poetry, grants and awards coming in,
contests and prizes proliferating. The wise grey consensus
counsels a return to the classics.

Meanwhile, poor salmon-scientist holds extinction
in a palmful of numbers
with nothing but data
to howl with.

Triangulation

With salmon stacked to the door, she squishes through fish,
boots tracking scales in the wheelhouse, across the galley floor,
down the companionway, and into the engine room.
By the end of the day, scales on the starboard fuel tank,
scales on the mast, deck winch, ladder, and steps. Scales
in her hair, in her gloves, up her sleeves, behind her ears.
Scales like freckles. Scales like raindrops. Like bindis,
like dragon skin. Scales in her eyes like contact lenses. Scales
flake. Scales stick fast as glue. Scales flash like diamond chips,
like glow-in-the-dark stars on the ceiling. Fairy dust your first
girlfriend wore on the last day of school. Piñata candy licked
with rust-colored tongues. Scales that taste like caviar,
like salt, like sperm, musty crush of ocean and stink of lust.
These scales. You lucky bastard, you don't even know,
but for each she scrubs and scrapes and cleans away,
she dreams your fingers drumming softly on her skin.
In the shower, she dreams your fingers into streams,
into stars that see, into mist, smoke, fire that breathes.
Your fingers hum whole notes on the bass clef of her back
or sweep window lips in warm breeze or win fast bets
in a hailstorm of desire. Those fingers smell like diesel,
like danger, like a damp, darling copy of her body. They chart
scars like ocean trenches, flit on her wrist as a seabird skims sky.
They snap buttons on a birthday suit, crank the wrong wrench,
the right wrench, and a screwdriver that turns everything
loose. Fingers like ants, the crumbs they hunt, and sugar
they love. Fingers round as butter, as cream, as you scream
into a cornfield from a car full of flesh. She dreams your fingers
on fleece, on flannel, on copper, on cotton, on nipples,
on knees. How can I compare? I love her the way a king's
black mouth gapes for air, the way any salmon will taste
the whole ocean and still turn for home.

PAMELA HOBART CARTER

Suquamish Waters

A painting by Alfredo Arreguín

above the Suquamish waters full of stars
where pelicans flap through a jeweled night

. . . fingered waves froth

fish   swifts   distant suns
all toss aloft
all spangly

. . . how right this dotted sky of scales
of green and glow
orange and crimson
where orcas dance

. . . every people   every thing gleams
crystalline   atomic
built of tiny other things
we cannot often see

MICHELE BOMBARDIER

Ascension, 1983

First bought artwork

Decades later, the picture still hangs
above our bed. Two salmon swim in tandem
with noses tilted suggesting their return
upriver. Two small beings, side by side.
They shimmer blue-green, their scales reflecting

sunlight under water. I think of us, wildly young,
believing in buoyancy, that love would protect us
from God knows what. The fight against the current.
Our do-or-die devotion. Reeling now when I consider
the years, the battering that we've survived.

Look: every fall bodies of salmon litter the riverbed
after their passage. At night I dream of fish scales
in sunlight. The glory of a lived life. Water
over rock. I did it. I'm swimming. I hear nothing
but the roar of the river in my ears.

KELLI RUSSELL AGODON

Ladders

When I think of escaping,
I think of rivers, salmon
mixing eggs with stones.

For weeks we watched them
from a sizzling fire pit,
watched silver glimmer

and slowly die. *Yes*, you said,
life is this. A fin in the sunlight
and the movement stops.

In other religions, we return
as the firefly, the ram, the elephant.
In my religion, I'm caught

between worlds, between an airy
cloud or burning cellar.
There is no hope for returning

as anything but a ghost.
We play with the souls in limbo,
talk to them with our Ouija board,

try to spy them in the corner
of the room. See that flame flickering?
It's an unbaptized baby, a saint

without a name. Tell me there are
better ways to pray. Tell me
as we watch the salmon swim

upstream how the song from
your guitar is a vesper to the river.
Isn't the song the salmon carries

in its scales enough? Isn't music
enough to make the fire pit respark,
to once again burn through the night?

NANCY CANYON

O Lady of the Salmon Run

O Lady of the flailing salmon,
is that you stirring the death-strewn
waters, wielding fish ladder in hand?
You are no mythic Lí Ban praying

to become a salmon and swim eastward
sea to sea—you are Our Lady of eggs
and milt, scouring gravel for nests,
sheltering redds from rain and wind.

O Lady, let the alevins survive
to grow into parrs. Show mature smolts
the course downstream to sea. In time,
guide the fishers' catch, leaving

abundant salmon for the killer whales.
O Lady, let the dead not go to waste—
please feed the cedars of the forest,
the insects, birds, and soil. The people's

voices will honor you with their songs
of praise. Won't you step out ahead?
We will follow in our wellies and
raincoats, trusting your guidance.

CINDY VEACH

A Case for the Canonization of Salmon

If I could saint one thing
it would be salmon.

For their sense of direction
the way they can always

find their way home.
For their ability

to swim upstream, persevere
and prevail over the will

of a river. For entering the world
parentless and then, smolted

against predators, make their way
to the sea. For entering that sea,

young, juvenile, going deep down
into uncharted darkness

staying there for the longest
least understood part of their lives

then returning to spawn
where they were spawned.

For the going out. For the coming
back. For the sea of living.

Anadromous

My father is a marine biologist,
So I grew up with legends of fish, their silvery bodies
Swimming sleek through water like parted glass.
He studies salmon, so we made the yearly pilgrimage
To Bonneville, where sturgeon rest like silent giants in their pool
And salmon fight in concrete beds and struggle through ladders.
That is how I remember them: fiery red and thrashing in a manmade lake,
Competing for food pellets flung from a six-year-old's chubby fist.

Only later did I find out how they die:
Their lives in the ocean, breathing in salt,
Abruptly close
As they journey up their natal streams
To dig holes in the riverbed for their redds,
To spawn perfect eggs,
To die upon the nursery's door
So that they may nurture the earth they owe fealty to.

No one knows how they know their way, what
Biological instinct guides them back to their roots
As bodies whither and food is abandoned.
I drive along the winding gorge to my childhood home
And wonder what it must be like
To wake with the knowledge of one's grave—to taste it in one's teeth.

When salmon swim home do they hear execution drums
Or the roar of flickering lifeblood
Competing with the rush of the water?
Do they know they are about to die,
Their bones sinking into the smooth rocks
Among their pearlescent young?

Or do they know only the familiar weight inside them,
That soaring right-wrongness
Of returning to a place you can only remember?

On the highway, the rain pours its cacophony along the cement stream.
I have an hour left to go
Until the cityscape swells and I walk through that once-familiar door.
And maybe it feels like this.

ALEX C. EISENBERG

Returning

Head lamps still pressed
forgotten against our foreheads,
dirty jewel-colored jumpers
wrapped round hungry bellies,
we sit at the steakhouse
hearts filled but hanging heavy
over our aching arching spines
and rubbed-raw ribs. The other ones
—marinating on her plate—she takes
and dangles from foul fingers
drips onto unnapkined lap
as her mouth rips
into meat and marrow.

I partake of the suburban salmon
all the while remembering the wild ones
still chugging up the Chiwawa
where we woke for weeks to witness
chum and sockeye spawn. Like eagles
we watched from the cliff as they splashed
and dashed their way upstream
til one morning, jealous, I slipped
my own shining body into the river
and dove down, arms glued to my side
snaking and shaking against the flow.

Under the relentless flash of LCD TV
people from other tables watch
our chaos-eyes, our cracked cackling
our ungoverned hunger
with suspicion but also starvation
for a taste of what we've seen
while those once-wild beasts

maimed and tamed
sliced neatly on their plates
grow cold
no longer an adequate answer
to the ache.

MARY MCMINN

Passionate Water Poem

I know you don't like the use of the word,
it's out of style, in disfavor,
but I have no other way of saying
my soul is drawn towards water—
    cool, clear, clean water.

My soul is drawn towards the order
that is water, the cyclic circularity of water.

I am dream towards water.
I swim and dive,
chuckle and jive
in water—
clear, cool water.

I live and play
make home all day
in water—cold, clear water.

I fight in stream,
dream salmon dreams in water.
Clear, cool, clean water.

SARAH STOCKTON

Salt and Other Spells

Inspired by the spawning cycle of
salmon in the Dosewallips River

We were water once
cyclical, transforming
salt and sediment into scales
anadromous

moving from sea into sweet water
catadromous
fresh to salt
to spawn, traveling

in deep-sea channels
transitioning
from silvery blue
to darker, going home

as we, floundering at water's edge,
turn in four directions
three visions, seven cycles,
bowing to salmon slipping through water

DUANE NIATUM

The Salmon

Mother of salt and slate,
foam and storm, eye of columbine;
sea flower carried by our shadow people
in a canoe on a horizon of mud and slime,
under the forest floor;

mixer of scale, bone and blood,
nose of Thunderbird who answered her
wave as it passed our rainbow mountain;
mother of calm and deliverance,
the tongue's drum from the cliff.

High above the raven valleys
near the sea, dream fox with the thread
of the current in its mouth touches
the Elwha River twice as she nestles
her eggs in the gravel.
The roots of the wind's hair builds
the birth cradle out of moon and tide.

Salmon Woman, a streaky thrust
at fertility, edges like Dawnmaker up
the slope, the thinning trail of the river.
Fever rattle of joy and tenacity,
gills bellow fullness and emptiness:
the songs of grandmothers
around Hadlock village fires that wove
our daughters into blankets
and water dreamers.

Dressing

Some women are bone with glitter in the eye;
Others are flesh and speak of the skin.

Toward the ocean, there is a show:
she aligns the twig and light.
What is in the hand dresses the woman.
What is in the eye covers her soul.

At Shi Shi, she stoops in the salal,
winds spiderweb around her fist
to string across, to close the wound.

At Kalaloch, she picks lichen from the black limb,
counts fern spores on the underside,
pulls the skillet of the afternoon sun over her head.

At Cape Alava, she stands off trail in the bog.
Cedar steeps, rain pours; the river fills with tannin.
At Cape Johnson, the ocean sips and throws white foam.
Pebbles rabble in its belly.

Salmon run the Hoh opening: pressed to the shelf,
the Olympics rebound gigantically.
Still, close, under her eye, traced by her hand,
salt and ice form, salmon flash silver in her net,
and the brocade of gray tatters
fades into the constant bluster of rain and wind.

LESLIE WHARTON

The Miracle

They say back in the day
you could walk across the river
on the backs of Salmon.
Like Jesus.
They say Jesus walked on water.
Maybe Jesus walked on the backs
of Salmon.
Maybe Salmon are the miracle.

DOTTY ARMSTRONG

Communion

Shore to shore
the Skykomish is awash with salmon
charging toward home.
I settle on the bank
eyeing a large one in the shallows
close to me.
She is red and ragged.
She is not digging her nest,
she is not turning on her side
flapping her tail to smooth the gravel,
she is not rolling out her eggs
in all directions. She is as quiet
as a night with no wind.
She is resting from her pilgrimage,
which has torn her up.
It is enough that I can join with her
in rest.

LAUREN SILVER

i'm a fisherman

within that one sentence
is his life story and
the story of his people and
the story of the salmon

the water; the salmon; the whales

they course through
his every cell
since he was
as he says
a little, little boy

he fished with his father
with his grandfather
all over this miracle place
we call home

the weaving
of the salmon
and the whales
and the water
and the heart of his people
they are all woven
together

GEORGIA JOHNSON

Before I Knew Salmon

For Brian Cladoosby

We drifted down from Edgewater Park—
no motor, river time, the river took our time.
There were places where the river gave us
back only our faces,
other places silver backs rose up so close
to meet us, then left us topside
with only the air to breathe.
The sun made its tattoo on us for that moment.

Another bend,
a row of boats,
sleep   ing   fish   er   men
Soft water voices,
"You ladies need hep?
Sittin' kinda low there."

The river turns on itself, and wheeling, we come
out from under a full canopy of alder
and see him.

Keeping the sleeping fishermen sleepy.
Standing at the bow like heron poised for catch,
head tilted, then bent as he bows in prayer posture,
true to his work.
He brings the net in, gathering those fish
like his daddy's daddy's daddy.

No one stands between them
only he counts the corks—

only he names the fish—
gently like beads on a rosary they rise
up and out of the water.

We came alongside and he gave us
a silver for our dinner,
like his daddy's daddy's daddy did.

BETHANY REID

Wild, Sacred

The year feels like one of those big container ships
out at sea, cumbersome, hard to turn.
Here we are, mid-August,
slowing down and cranking the wheel
toward autumn. In the ditches
near my house, the weeds grow wan
and leggy, a few pink, five-petaled blossoms
winking up. Or not pink,
but pinkish. Salmon colored. Off Picnic Point,
salmon flipper around so easily, not
cumbersome. I take out my phone and look up
my pinkish flower. Weren't we just now speaking
of the sacred in all creation?
In weeds, in us, in the salmon?
My wildflower blessing the ditch
beneath Doug fir and western red cedar
is called herb Robert, also Robert geranium,
crow's foot, squinter-pip, fox geranium,
kiss-me-quick, knife and fork,
stinking Robert, stinking Bob,
Saint Robert's herb, and death-come-quickly,
though the notes say it isn't deadly.
Good for warding off stomach ailments
as well as deer and rabbits from the garden.
A French monk named Robert
cataloged its uses around 1000 AD.
No smart phone in his pocket. No handy app
with an Adam-like facility for naming things.
Did monk Robert know salmon?
Were his years as cumbersome as ours?

Sacrifice

Do you remember your first fishing trip?
                    beneath warm rubber tires
        Crunching gravel
                            beneath creaking planks
        Trickle of the soothing stream

        Whispers from tall grasses
            as   your legs whooshed by

Was it then you saw them?
        The strongest fish you'd ever seen
        Swiftly swishing tails,

                    S
                L L
            I   I
            C   C
        I   I
        N   N
    G   G
                    through the surface

Was it then you smelled them?
        Musty | Wet | Churned-Up Silt
        Fainting wafts of ocean's salt
        Scales cleansed in fresh snowmelt

Was it then you noticed them?
        Spawning

        S l o w   i   n   g

                    floating
        Sinking and floating
        Sinking

        Did you honor their sacrificial ceremony?
Will you now?

BILL YAKE

The Salmon of Green Cove Creek

Silver at sea,
       bright as breaking waves, flashes
that—in aging—turn to shadows
       of moss
              green darting through
                     ravines
of forest and hard rain.

I have come down to the stream gingerly,
       through a tunnel of devil's club,
              to lean
       on a walking stick now braced in mud,

              to greet and watch
                     the water move.

Salmon, chum—marked and blazed as if
       by muted sunlight that once
              worked and weaved
                     its sodden way through
       cedar boles—
they rest and thrash, insist upstream.

Dowsed-undulations congregate,
       engage in furtive, then blatant
              unisons.

Flames they are that, when cooled,
                 quiver against the generative flex,
                      the roil,
                 plash and shiver,
                      to collapse ecstatic

into a whole and circular moment—
          inverted and dying into fertility.

Sojourn

GABRIELA DENISE FRANK

(yubəč / chinook)

O
ǧdə uʔ sʔuladxʷ
/ first salmon / O queen
of fishes / in pregnancy, an erasure of
self   a new being born, both miracle & meat / a handwoven
net of   living threads lovingly encircle what cannot possibly be held, what will
eventually   move through it / we think back through our mothers if we are women / we are each other's
keystones / lose one & the bridge collapses / building bodies is a slow process: set the spine, lay the bones, the muscles
the gills, the fins / sx̌ay̓ay, čəlkadiʔ, sk̓ʷubič, sčətšad / for the fortunate ~ 100 in 10,000 ~ the world begins / in a red pearl
/ a yolk sac nourishes the newly hatched / alevin to fry / thus begins the grand drift downstream / flotsam, jetsam / one
creature to another / from redd we parr, we smolt, we molt in brackish water / part salt, part fresh / we become ancestors
breath by breath / eight precious years etched in strontium deep in the bone / each ring a journey, estuary to ocean,
dxʷk̓ʷiƛ̓əb to   x̌ʷələč / chiseled in otolith / we shelter in kelp forests / the Moon spins in the gullet, whirling
between   hard palate & soft / a glowing orb (insouciance) around which life turns / beware
the jack-   light hovering above the tricksy abyssal with false promises of feast—feast, O queen, O
chum,   while   you
can.   ~   ~

Leap!
dear children: swim
vast distances, forge upstream, seek   a savage
intuition of the self \ let everything happen to you   beauty
& terror ~ keep going ~ no feeling is final \ we look at the world once   in child-   hood, the
rest is memory \ a turning, a volta \ toxin, tocsin, clinamen \ a swerve of atoms, blue to gold,   silver to brown \
(magic) the body's semelparous intelligence, a siren call upstream \ strumming, drumming, clanging on the kype, the hook,
the   peal, the song spurts inner yearning to milt, to drench, to spread the self thick with possibility \ the lustrous redd-scent
becomes nourishment \ (who can say which meal is their last?) \ some guard buried treasures 'til their dying
~day \ others hunt for one last companion \ does it sting less, knowing our cells dwell on in motes & mosses, herbs & shrubs, trees
& insects, songbirds & bears? (consolation) sewn into our descendants' memories: a billion glit-   tering gold disks,
the Pilchuk afire with sunset \ purple camas flowers shouting from the banks \ north wind   fragrant with
earth & sweet pollen & acrid leeks \ an imprint set (future's shimmering glimpse)   settles into
oblivion, scale by scale \ our ghosts remembered yet   unknown \   come, fry:
the journey itself is   your home·   ~   ~
~

33

SIERRA NELSON

Self-Portrait as Spawner

You should have seen me in my Ocean Phase, salty and silver.
But weren't we all just an eyed egg once?
We're always changing, we just forget.

Now I'm a little longer in the cycloid,
my odolith has been around the block.
You look to my speckles. Do I have a black tongue?

Am I wearing a ring, adipose fin clipped?
You think you know me.
Hot tip: even if I don't turn red, I've changed.

So what if I grow a hook or a hump?
It's hard work getting a redd ready.
I'm putting on my tiger stripes, I'm putting on my gold.

But not to get caught by *you*. Do you know how many depressions
I had to rest in, how many logs I leaped, to believe in love again?

Cast Long

In memory of Suzanne, the hopeful one

You laid on that damn bed
Cottony blue eyes half-closed
Spine curled like a barbed hook
And asked me to take you fishing.

So let's go, my deep-sleep beauty
    Of powdered bones and sage-burnt prayer.
Let's run to the river,
Dodge the brown cows
That chase us over the bank
    Into the pigweed, gold and orange
Lures clinking,
Laughing too loud in too-big waders
Squooshy from splats of dung
    Steaming in the October chill.

The skank of fish rot hits us like a fist
So sour it's sweet
Bodies everywhere
Eyes plucked by crows and gulls
Flies feeding in pockets of flesh
The birds scream
When will we leave?

Ack! Black! The color of death
That follows the slow bruise of longing
    For a life soon gone.

Across the river, the alders
    Are hung like Christmas trees
    With the lures of unlucky fishers.
Not us, Suzanne. Not you.

Shhhhh. Step in slowly.
Watch the water radar off our boots
Bigger and bigger circles
Searching something wild.

When up the stream
Comes the big-scaled king,
Humping high rocks in the low current
Smelling home and sex and death,
Its great green back cutting
A white V toward us.

Cast easy, cast long
Cast fast, cast away your sins, Sister,
   On the slow roll of river
Where a tug on a light line
Can raise the dead.
And oh! The salmon's quick silver side
Catches the white light of fall.

CHRIS GUSTA

The Endless Ladders

The young salmon's life
is not such a struggle.
Who needs help
moving with the current?
There are no pills
for moving with ease.

It's only with
the struggle back that
the professionals come in—
the Wellbutrin,
the therapy,
the endless ladders.

Why don't they teach us
to jump when we're young?

Maybe they're trying
but we're only interested
in seeing the open waters
until we are haunted by heredity.

TITO TITUS

A Salmon of a Man

Them salmon fish is mighty shrewd. They got senators and politicians, too.
Just about like the president. They run every four years.

Woodie Guthrie, "Talking Columbia"

Salmon-in-the-heat-of-season
attack shimmering rapids, cascades,
cataracts, foaming pearlescent rivers;
in sunlight they crash on watery boulders,
flop into cold pools, regain, and do it again.

Silver rocket bodies slap backward,
leap anew, briefly shine like speeding
almond-shaped mirrors, briefly brilliant,
splash back, lunge forward, up toward
their Purpose again and again. Yet again.

      That's like us, isn't it?
      Well, maybe sometimes.

Few complete the journey,

fewer today than before.
It's a tough trip—hypocaustic seas; asphalt,
combustion-engine lead, arsenic,
mercury, and copper leach to creeks,

forever chemicals from factories;
pesticides, herbicides, fertilizers
from farms that feed us; and
blockading dams with hot reservoir waters.
Still—some survive:

sockeye, coho, Chinook, pink,
and chum charge the rocky gauntlets—
bears, seals, orcas, and humans
drift fishing, side drifting, plunking, trolling,
casting spinners, wobblers, and spoons.

We hit the shoals of life, you and I,
sometimes jagged and strewn—dashed dreams,
our own, which we call *revised aspirations;*
we abandon teen dreams—once reasonable,
now preposterous; or we decide

we don't want what *almost impossible* demands—
or so it seems when we find a pleasant pond,
a good life, something stable and safe.
Like less-endowed salmon, we end up in pools,
riverside bars, lower elevation eddies

in life's migration. Brando in *The Waterfront*
reminds us—*we could've been contenders.*
In small ponds, koi circle 'round, pay no mind.
My great-great-grandfather never knew
whether his sperm survived.

       But Alexander the Great?
       Helluva salmon, that one.

Lobster

I am a lobster
And everyone around me,
they say "well all salmon go upstream
this time of year"
And they say I'm a salmon
I believe them
So I try to go upstream
But I'm a lobster
Lobsters do not go upstream
I'm not bad at what I do
I'm a great lobster
But they say to me "how can a
salmon
not swim upstream?"

AUDREY MILLER

Evolution from Salmon

Hey
Hey you
You want to swim, don't you?
You want to glide like we do
Synchronized through the ocean's shoes

Hey
Hey you
What're you trying to do?
Get your mind back into your flippers
And swim like we do

Hey
Hey you
Get off the sand you goof
Are you trying to dance like we do
But on the land so deadly to you?

Hey
Hey you
Are you in denial of what's true?
We are salmon that swim in the ocean's shoes
Not flesh balls with feet and tails that swoosh

Hey
Hey you
You've learned the ways but deny them and pursue
A life that isn't pure and replace it with a life that is new
You've learned to crawl, cradle, and chew
But can you still swim, like us salmon can do?

Hey
Hey you
Turns out you can swim too
We're still better, though, better than you
You'll see, later or soon

Hey
Hey you
Have you forgotten we are watching you?
Growing your fleshy land army that can walk like you do?
You grab them with your hands from the ocean and as they make their debut

Hey
Hey you
There's too dang many of you!
Swinging from the trees we'll never swing to
Playing and enjoying yourself and crying your hoots

Hey
Hey you
Fine, fine, do what you do
We don't care, we never do
Just please don't take all the salmon, will you?

JONATHAN WENT

Sojourn

There have been many days
now I have not tasted
the salt of ocean freedom.
The dreams I have obstructed
by incalculable odds:
the rural small town.
The doubt, always
a predator I have
to watch for. I was taught
to never accept myself.
My queer nature
the source of so much
harm. This is what white
men like my father do
to the good body: seize
it, dam the abundance.
Make a square farm.

All my life
I have fought for survival.
I say, I want to give up.
You say, what would you have

if you were not proud
of your florid body,
its red and green colors?
You have fattened at the edges
of a teeming universe.
The journey home lies
in this: the claim
of your one wild heart.

ARIANNE TRUE

Diadromous

This fall, which is every fall,
            the salmon will return to the stream behind my house.
They will wait in the Sound until a high enough tide
to make the trip up through the estuary,
where crows and gulls pick the eyes out of carcasses,
and through the culvert that, when I was small,
I could fit through but feared. I did walk it once,
sixteen. Young feet unsure in the murk, pants rolled
above the knees but still wet from the splash. My
friend ahead of me, all pressure and shame. But
I did make it through to where the salmon,
in the fall, will wait to jump their first
jump upstream in our creek. I made it back, too,
to the beach where the gulls toss young crabs and
chase each other. Last time I was there, I checked
the culvert and it seems small now, impossible for
my teenage body, only broken glass and spiders.

When they make that jump, the salmon keep swimming
up, pausing in pools. Their bodies move like current,
you can almost see the water inside them. Their bodies
are half-gone, some, in the missing chunks and peeling
skin. Did you know salmon don't eat on their way home?
They metabolize their tissues, like a tree keeping warm
burning its branches. This whole time, it's all smell. Memory
of scent guides them back, though it's been years.
When they are young and leaving the stream, ocean-
bound, they turn one last time to look home, and let
every scent of it wash through their bodies, I mean
literally wash through their porous bodies, to remember.

I moved home last year. I don't mean to Seattle,
I mean to the neighborhood I grew up in. Have

been avoiding, perhaps, at times. My city changes
so fast, and memories overlay developments
until I don't know what I'm seeing, or when. But
this part of town is the same as when I left. There
are still so many old trees, tall or gnarled, even
from my new window. Most of the houses are still
houses somehow, and the roads are still wide
and quiet. The sidewalks still cracked where
heavy roots break them. I can see the mountains
from the ridge, and from the same spot
turn around and see the grocery store's high tower like
a foam car-antenna ball stories above the parking
lot, which is still a strip mall of businesses
whose signs have watched me grow up,
the same neon. For a while,
I didn't think I could come home to here. But
this is where we could afford, and something
said, "come back," said, "rest a while. stay."
I am a poor planner but I trust my nose.
Can sniff out home when the rivers
look the same meeting the sea. These open streets.
Looking up the same trees, whose branches silhouette
above the low rooflines. The freight trains, sonorous
and uneven when they call up these same hills,
catch up to my legs and their older, strong steps.
Walking the same trails down the ravine to see
the salmon return every fall, and finally this fall.

NIMISHA MONDAL

The Search for Home

have you ever wondered
how new salmon populations came to be?

fresh rivers, now full, but once upon a time
not one salmon called them home

queens of navigation arrived in these new homes
with goals for returning home, elsewhere

have you ever pondered
on that first salmon arriving?

she was most certainly looking for her birthplace
as salmon do, seeking home to birth the next generation

this was not it
was she lost?

have you ever thought to be like this first salmon,
a lost one that will lead the way?

her scales will never cast a reflection
upon the history books, she will only shine

here in the river ripples, twisting and leaping,
laughing, as we strain to read the map before us

way finding in cold waters, despair
throwing barriers higher than the rapids

unaware when the waters warmed, map frayed
beyond recognition, hope for home lost

like our queen, we may lay down our weary load
spawning whatever will come

fading as we lay our bodies
down upon the rocks

fading, even as we become the first,
the ancient, the ancestors, for this new place

let us all seek to be like the lost salmon
be not weary of your search for home

search for it like it is your life calling
for it is your life calling

but do not despair when the home you find
is not the home you left

you may indeed be destined to create new worlds,
a home your kind has not yet dared to dream of

MAIAH MERINO

Rainbow streams

if I wear a rainbow
riding your back
falling into streams

splashing with the
others a drop
or ocean to see

I could go back
home—where my
nana's dust is

swimming as fast
and as furious as
your Salmon family
                    returning

in the city
you burn
when the sun shines on an
oil patch

                    against the blacktop

like the stenciled
fish close to the drains
your presence remains

                    a part of us.

ANNE MURPHY

A Rainy Day Is

salmon language gathering sound.
Rhythms rush the stream
whose banks stretch to contain excitement,
flooding the bay with a signature call
discernable to family fish
in their saline cycle
feeding in ocean spirals.
Hillsides lend tenor,
rolling gravel a muffled percussion,
mud-bottom bay the hum
that salmon feel along their bodies.
Their silver cymbals flash a knowing—
there is no journey
without the song of home.

Homecoming (in heat)

Anadromous
Species returning home

Overcoming
Surge upon
Surge of
Oncoming currents

Granted reprieve and respite
In irregularities of
Rivers' edges

"How long is Britain's
Coastline?" asked
Benoit Mandelbrot—

Seen from the salmon's perspectives
The infinite recesses
Render Euclidean geometries
Moot

Unless they are superimposed by
Outside forces
Seeking to stamp rigidity in
Unending searches for energy—

Glowering overhead into
Transmission lines
To feed energy hungry
Appetites

The sprites appear
To remind
And inspire

By the hearth of
The fires
That heat the
Blessings of
The Salmon

Please don't turn up the heat
Too much
Before they arrive
Home.

JON NEHER

Redfish Lake

High in weathered ranges
An indigo lake ripples
In adiabatic wind, where
Amid green reeds
And tawny banks
Two redfish claim
The continent

Monumental sockeye
Nine hundred miles run
Cataract and canyon
Haul up six thousand feet
From a distant sea, migration
Tough enough for burly geese
They make this lake
Or die

But the little redfish kokanee
The sockeye's closest kin
Chose this mountain lake
To be their sea
Stay the bitter winters
Under a yard of ice
And come the summer
Trundle up flat Fishhook Creek
Perhaps a meager mile
To spawn

I watch the redback kokanee
From a weathered bridge
As traveler and tourist

In my own sockeye season
And wonder
Why the little fish
Look so remarkably
Content

At Dusk, Salmon Spawn

Chum know where home shines and the quest,
leave seas behind and roaming years.
Rise moon, spin filigrees of silver flesh.

Each fall return, numbers small and pressed
to streams of birth they churn and veer.
Chum know where home shines and the quest.

Ancient cycles spawn but with same zest?
Autumn rot of carcasses sears
rise moon, spin filigrees of silver flesh.

Fish the size of good men's arms and chests
fight through snags and silt, I hear.
Chum know where home shines and the quest,

they rest and nest in still pools ever west
with great heaves strike shore weary.
Rise moon, spin filigrees of silver flesh.

Spawn, thrash, and flop then silent, ever rest
providence for loam, beaver, and deer.
Chum know where home shines and the quest,
rise moon, spin filigrees of silver flesh.

SETH GOLDSTEIN

At the New Year

At the new year
Each fall, we return.

Crossing doorways to fill pews
Rising and falling
To sing words of atonement and celebration.
Expressing longing and gratitude
We seek to transform to
Better versions of ourselves.

The liturgists had it wrong.
We are not sheep but salmon
Passing beneath the staff,
Tagged and recorded.
Making our way from ocean to river to creek
Against the flow and over obstacles
To arrive at the same place.
Appearances changed by time and experience
At the intersection of life and death
We fulfill a sacred obligation and desire to create and re-create.

It is difficult for us
To approach this yearly ritual of practicing mortality.
To demonstrate commitment
To profess confession and regret
To understand that life is lived not as a current but an eddy.

Were we truly like the salmon.
Acting with innate knowledge of the way,
And understanding the necessity of return.
Recognizing that building a redd is a prayer.
Content with the idea that charity is sowing the seeds we will never see sprout.
Content knowing that what we do feeds the future.

JILL MCCABE JOHNSON

Bedded in Wet Rock Like Any Other Roe

Bedded in wet rock like any other roe,
I woke in a float at river's rim.

Sweet slurry of ancestors,
my pillow and pledge.

I dreamed down current,
a hatchling of spring's surprise.

Fry to smolt, I weltered
in fluvial estuaries and brackish tides.

When vast waters welcomed me,
our sweep of Chinook synchronized.

Outline of orcas. Shape of shark.
Such mercury molting.

We skirted the surf in a cross weave
of silver, bolting lightning back at the sky.

Rest wriggled in a forest of eelgrass.
Porphyra camouflaged our flash.

We swam hard against the waves—
building muscle, storing steam

—till the ancestors called us
from a spill of snow-fed waters.

Clear slipstream of memory.
River me home. River me home.

CYNTHIA R. PRATT

Sampling Summer Chum on the Dosewallips

Light dances between scattered
spray, lithe as a hummingbird.
The fish plows forward against my boots,
my polypropylene shins,
as I walk upstream through cobbled riffles.

Her tail lashes back and forth,
dorsal fin cutting the air.
Each thrash digs into the riverbed
as she fills the redd with eggs,
then drifts away, spent, ready to die.

Scales float by in the shallows
next to another female's body,
gills still moving.
Watching where I step,
I count the concave disks of gravel,
riverbed's pocked cheeks, holding my own body
back from the current, the shattered
limbs of trees, those unseen logs a death trap.

This purple-green, striped fish,
lying on her side, shudders,
a movement so faint
it could be lapping water,
or reflections bouncing
from the morning sun.

Up ahead, three more fish,
one a skin-ripped, hook-jawed male.
Then two more, too quick to identify,
slide by, driven by instinct.
In the way, I wobble for balance.

A bald eagle sits on a tree snag
waiting for this intruder to leave.
What happens today, or any day, is not
mine to give or take away.

The eagle swoops, talons extended,
lifts the chum I just eased past me
up into the canopy of cedars.

ED STOVER

Uncle Les and I

Uncle Les and I
are fishing for trout
in the cold mountain waters
of the American River
near where we live.
I'm sixteen years old
and am spin fishing,
casting my lure from the bank,
slowly reeling it in.

I'm in my bathroom shaving,
eighty-two years old,
with no good reason
to remember that late summer day
such a long time ago.
Yet here it is and there I am—
casting, reeling, casting, reeling
without getting a strike.

That's when I see it
slowly finning in the shallows
below the bank
on the far side of the river—
a monster fish,
broad sides glowing red,
its single eye facing me
black, opaque, mysterious.

The fish seems weary,
its hooked jaws gasping,
head scarred and battered.
Then, as I watch,
it rolls to its side and dies.

I stare and stare.
It is like watching a warrior die.
The massive armor of its body—
armor that has protected it
on the long journey from the sea—
flashes like a sword in the current,
then is carried away downstream.

Later I ask my uncle.
Coho—probably spawned out, he says.
He describes the age-old odyssey,
freshwater to saltwater,
the final return to home waters
to spawn and die,
the cycle of life complete.

Around me I feel the current—
pulling me, calling.

LAURA READ

In or Out

The thing everyone knows about salmon
is that they come home to die.
My brother came home from Japan
where he's lived for seventeen years.
He was always our mother's favorite, the baby,
born at the end of August
after a summer of her wearing either the red
sundress with the yellow flowers
or the blue one.
My other brothers played in the plastic pool,
the sprinkler a metronome, the screen door
banging open and closed.
In or out! Mom would yell
from the kitchen where she was making
sandwiches or cutting melons into half-moons
or mixing Country Time lemonade
in the plastic pitcher.
I can still hear the spoon.
I asked David if he remembered *In or out!*
Or *Having It or Not Having It*
which is what my brothers used to say
after Mom read them what was for hot lunch
the next day. Turkey with mashed potatoes
and those rolls that smelled good all morning
through Science and Language Arts.
Having It. But that was me.
David is fourteen years younger,
so I don't know how he felt about the rolls.
There is so much I don't know about David.
I haven't kept in touch.
I knew death early, so I have been furious
that he chose to be gone.

I didn't know that he remembered me,
the way I would leave the belly button
of the peanut butter intact and scoop
around it all the way down.
David's head used to get sweaty when he slept,
and I liked to pick him up and smell him.
This is how salmon remember their rivers.
When I was in college studying French
and David was in kindergarten, I called him
Mon Petit Chou, which means My Little Cabbage.
In all the years he's been gone,
I've walked by a house in my neighborhood
every night where a woman grows fantastic
cabbages. In late summer they are huge
and look so proud and private under the moon.
David has been gone so far and so long
and my missing him has turned into how
my son describes my face when I haven't
seen him for a while. Vaguely angry.
But now David wants to move home.
I have been here the whole time,
so I'm vaguely angry we're throwing him
a party. He tells my parents he needs
to come back because they are getting old
and draws an invisible knife across his neck.
How do salmon know when it's time?
David is coming back with his family,
but on this visit, he and I are alone.
One night, he asked me what it was like
after Terry died. I told him the whole thing:
how my son bent over at the waist
like he'd been kicked when I told him,
how it happened the day of the windstorm
so ten minutes after the call, the power
went out, how we slept upstairs all together
with flashlights under piles of blankets,
and I kept waking up and remembering

and trying to write the word *dead*
next to Terry's name in my mind,
and David listened until I was finished
and then said, *I'm sorry I missed so much time.*

TRAVIS WELLMAN

Until It Be Laid There

Her pearls stowed with tenderest of care
Among the pines within the glist'ning thrum
While hunger rests until it be laid there

Though courted by kypes, those prognathic snares
Who tasseled to her freckled tail be strung
Her pearls stowed with tenderest of care

She joins the doomed ranks who slalom to bears
Who by besieged falls lay wait thereupon
As hunger rests until it be laid there

Neath fierce and noble grizzly does she stare
From boiling froth as her eyes gauge the rung
Her pearls stowed with tenderest of care

From that cauldron's churning precipice where
By hell's mouth her silver fuselage flung
While hunger rests until it be laid there

Though noble snouts would in long night despair
That tumid keel shan't greet their patient tongue
Her pearls stowed with tenderest of care

Rubies glisten about her shallow cairn
Yet even as her swan song as last sung
Her pearls stowed with tenderest of care
While hunger rests until it be laid there

CHRISTEN MATTIX

Record Salmon Run

In the depths, I glimpse them,
grey shadows that flicker
or rest under the log bridge:
a kind of effortless hovering
(gills open and close)
in the circular act of breathing.

Then turning flint faces,
they muscle their way up,
silver scales glinting in sunlight,
agony of sheer will, sheer toil,
flounder up fall, or flip—

       A moment's flight broken
by rocks
               tossed
                        in roiling waters,
gashed
          on sharp snags.

I wonder how they go
without eating,
leave the ocean
without hope of return,
die without seeing their young,
follow the magnetic pull of home.

VICTORIA DOERPER

When I See the Salmon Run in Padden Creek

I weep for every twist of torn silver,
Every ragged scale, every backslide
And battering leap against concrete
Of fish ladder or jagged edge
Of low-water exposed rock.
I see sandy, hollowed-out hiding places,
The curved, scraggly bodies at temporary rest
Before the next attempt
To struggle forward,
Back to the place of birth,
A place of coming spawn
And sure death after that,
The long yearning,
Fresh to salt, salt to fresh,
Salt of the tears I cannot stop
Watching salmon
Make their way, against odds
Of dogs, raccoon, bear, eagle,
Following the harrowed route
Of a salmon's ancestral fate,
Their leap into destruction
And the future.
I stand here
In slack-jawed awe,
Witness to their faith
And sacrificial gift,
A glimpse of my kin,
A glint on their waters.

Invisible Thread

KATE REAVEY

feathers of a jay
tiny, sewn, precise—
tomorrow a salmon will rise
toward this imagined nourishment

KATHRYN TRUE

moss bright river flows
while salmon spirit shimmers
deep within heartwood

BARBARA HERSEY

Big river harnessed
breaks hearts who love wild salmon
darkness light obscures

JOHN S GREEN

dammed rivers
these teardrops
not enough

LINDA CONROY

if life were sacred
we would not mess the passage
for the fish and fowl
we'd work to free ourselves
from greed

PETRO C. K.

watchful eyes
a Pacific salmon jumps
into a dataset

silent lightning
migrating salmon arcs
into a moon

BEVERLY ANNE JACKSON

Arduous journey
Fulfills salmon's destiny
Watching, we marvel.

RICHARD TICE

jumbled fish nets
a woman blesses the harvest
by kissing a salmon

DAVID BERGER

big salmon in the boat . . .
next day it grows
a foot

STEVE SCHINNELL

my taste for salmon is rather distinct
    in that i try to appreciate them
        without helping them become extinct

JACOB D. SALZER

crescent moon—
a glimpse of salmon
in the river's darkness

KATHLEEN TICE

salmon bake . . .
the crescent moon
low in the sky

CAROLE MACRURY

rainbow's end . . .
the purse seiner's net
drawn tight

GARY EVANS

starry night
salmon weave more
of an ancient fabric

salmon run . . .
returning more
than they took

salmon spawning
eaglets' screeches echo
among treetops

salmonspiritsabovebelowwithinbeyond . . .

TOM HAHNEY

muscling up the river
of their spawning—
spiderweb—autumn wind

JS NAHANI

Invisible thread
connects me to pink salmon
our uphill journey

MICHAEL MARTIN

Gravel circles, there
Where the water swirls around
Salmon spawning joy

MICHAEL DYLAN WELCH

Issaquah sunrise—
what's left of a salmon
reddening the creek

CATHY LEAR

Fabric

Silver thread flashes
Salmon, weaver of the world
Swims upstream to spawn

HANK MUSKA

Departed

O Salmon, what went wrong?
Where have you gone?
O Salmon, did no one care?
Is that why you are not there?

SHEILA SONDIK

Salmonology

Salmon sway, waiting in the shadows for the right moment to fling themselves into the churning waterfall. Making it all the way to the top appears impossible to me, but failure doesn't seem to be part of their equation. They leap, fall back, and leap again.

> after years in the depths—
> an urgent summons
> from a mountain stream

The native peoples understand, cherish, and celebrate the salmon, while relying on them as a crucial source of sustenance. The colonists viewed the environment as resources to exploit. Capitalism doesn't recognize or value the interdependence of all the facets of the bioregion. Indiscriminate logging and damming continue to threaten the salmon's way of life.

> convergent evolution
> orcas and humans share
> a taste for chinook

At odd moments, I find myself reflecting on the life and lore of these iconic fish.

> airport walkway—
> smolt swim downstream
> while small fry float backwards

Restoring their way of life will reward us with a healthier world for our own small fry.

> let the river run free the salmon

ROBERT SUND

Salmon Moon

Surf
of moonwave,
        mist of dawn by the sea.
Mist of long lovely night ending.

The moon steps through the night.
It goes out into the south and west.
Wind comes out of the south and west.

Between sparse old shoreland spruce
        the moon is a silver wing
                in the clouds.

All night
the clouds drift over.
All night, salmon gather—
first of the run.

Fish School

ELAINE MILLER BOND

salmon nurture trees nurture salmon nurture trees nurture salmon nurture trees nurture salmon nurture trees nurture

JUDITH ROCHE

Salmon Suite

The salmon's genius is in making friends with fate.

Tom Jay

Steelhead   January to May
Steelhead

Deep waders have found a vein
  to the heart of cold,
    the resplendence of river,
the grandeur of muscle
  and elegant economy of spirit.

They leave lives unattended,
  wives in childbed
    husbands in beery bars,
to step into swift waters.

They're there for the fight.
Wild winter-run spawners, steelhead
are trout on steroids, river's darlings,
  the prize at the end of every sea-slung

rainbow, not stay-at-homes
like their cousins, but heroes
on the romance of the journey.
  Deep waders understand this

at pre-lingual level. There are
many kinds of love in life.

Railbird, Copper Demon, Queen of the Waters,
Parmacheene Belle, Grizzly King,

Silver Doctor, Wet Spider, Princess,
          spoon and spinner.

The Samish, Stillagamish, Cowlitz,
Chehalis, Hoh, Humptulips, Nisqually,
Quinault, Skagit, Skykomish,
          Toutle, Washougal.

Flyline and cast,
          weight and diameter,
silk to monofilament. If spirit
is the fusion of thought and feeling

connecting one being to another,
and *kairos* a moment when everything
can change. Of the many,
          this is one kind of love.

Smolt   Mid-April to late July
Smolt

          Salmon travel backwards until they reach saltwater.

Being young, I don't know
          where I go.
I face my lake
          and float
          backward into my future.
Trembling on the edge
          of what I can't yet see,
          green-shadowed,
I go with water's flow and trust strange
          rapture singing in my blood,
          ride the river like a knife's edge.
Breathe and float
          oxygen and insect,
          cut and rise,

I've seen where I've been
        so, rehearse my return
tracing it in latticed strands
        recorded in starry lace
        fabric of night.

Current pulls me down
        to spill over smolt slide,
Plunge the plashy fall,
        slip the snap of gray bird's beak,

turn to face ocean opening flat and wide
        beyond imagining   no horizon,
        taste first fingers of bitter brine,
        flick silver and learn salt.
Because my throat itches
        I swallow what awaits me.
Begin young, I've cut my heart
        on the dream
        of the high seas.

Sockeye   *June to August (October)*
Celestial Navigation

       Salmon biologists are investigating the possibility
       that salmon find their way home by the stars.

I remember, I remember
the hollowed nest in stream of stars
the size of my eyes, I remember
the swell of water, shape
of light, celestial order to mirror
the song of river, the constellations
glitter into place to make the map—
       Scorpio, Virgo, Libra, Canis Major—
Sirius, the brightest, Orion, my own
clean cold water over stones, the whir

of the earth spinning through starry sky,
drag of tidewaters lifting
the estuary, sweet taste of reeds
and rushes, edged sedge grass
in dance with wind and water flow,
in silver pool pulsing scent,
deep home loam, the river
where I was born.

Chinook/Sockeye   August to September (October)
The River Dance

> *Aflame with the crimson color of marriage, the salmon*
> *Seek their lovers.*
> *For the salmon, the act*
> *Spinning out life*
> *Is an act of death*
> *For the salmon*
> *Life lives in death.*
> *The salmon bets its life on love.*

>> from *Salmon Coming Home in Search of Sacred Bliss,*
>> Mieko Chikappu

Choose the site for depth and current
        water flow and roll.
Turn, push and burrow gravel,
        deepen the redd.
Settle in to test the depth.
Busy while the males fight
        to get to me,
                the prize,
        my hope chest full of posterity.

I choose the reddest one—
        Aflame with the crimson color of marriage,
torn and tattered but flushing
        deep burgundy slash mark pattern.

I pass back and forth over him
      caressing his back and sides
            while the others drift away,
            all their fire fading to dull gray.

Crouching together we hover
      pulsing along the thin dark stripes,
      our lateral lines, sensing
            every quiver,
throbbing our ancient dance of love and risk.

Spinning out our lives
      we love each other to death.

Coho/Chinook/Sockeye   September to October (November)
Ghost Salmon

      The salmon die
      Ahh, so tenderly.

            from *Salmon Coming Home in Search of Sacred Bliss,*
            Mieko Chikappu

Everything draws down toward autumn
and the way light is broken in splintered color
      we are broken to feed the multitudes
            take, eat, this is my body
                  this is my blood
eagle and osprey
      raven and bear,
            stonefly and gull
                tear my flesh.
My silt settles and salts the stream
      cedar and fern,
            algae and fungi,
                amoeba and protozoa
                    suck a rich soup.

My body emptied of eggs,
     milky milt settled,
completing
    the circle,
        eelgrass and catkin,
          cougar and lynx,
creating life from the dead,
Food for the stream,
    I feed all comers.

CATHERINE KYLE

The Fish Ladder

In the basement of the Ballard Locks:
the fish-viewing room, window to a
world of urgent churning. Salmon climb
the ladder of turquoise blue, struggling
to rivers where they hatched.

Granddad often brought us here
when we were young, usually on free
parking days. Down we would go
to the cavern of concrete with the
square portals cut in its walls.

We would watch them, hands gripping
the cold guardrail. Watch their silver
scales flash like sabers. Pushing against
the punishing tide. All wriggling muscle
and wide eyes.

Granddad would point at some, huge
bites gouged from the hulls of their
glittering flanks. Still, those salmon
would press on, determined. Even
with ribbons of flesh trailing from

the spot where a seal or sea lion fed.
How many times have I thought
of this lesson and wondered just what
he was imparting? This was a man
who was shouldering depression,

divorce, and unemployment in the
cavern of his heart, though we could
not see in its windows clearly.
Did they mirror him somehow,
those fish that leapt ahead, despite

their missing chunks? Or was it
for us? Little wide-eyed grandchildren,
unknowing of the many teeth that
might take bites from us? I have
salmon days sometimes, days

where I feel that the current
I exist in might dissolve me. But I
think of him pointing, saying softly
with his eyes: *Keep going. You are
more than what you've lost.*

JENNIFER PRESTON

Lateral Lines

Fish have a sense organ called a lateral line located along both sides of their body. It is akin to having a sixth sense, where sight, hearing, and touch work together.

They have reached the ocean's end, turn-around-time.
The undeniable buried deep, brings them back.
With quiet longing, the salmon swim past the glittering
glass of western windows, their unseen inhabitants.

Below the ripples, red scales pulse and green flanks glisten,
they ripen and return, knowing their own river's current,
delivering that final, furious thunder in the shallows
of their birth.

At first, we hear a muscular defiance of water,
then see them pointing like arrows
aligned upstream.

We are awed into silence, longing for words
absent in English, thirsty for language that
reveals the sight of senses.
But there is a terrible drought—a dam.

Lateral lines of awareness converge
with effort, by jumping the channel.
Let us begin with this wonder—
*Tell me the name for the sound
of salmon tails slapping the riverbank?*

I will listen and keep watch,
shaping my lips to learn,
knowing that we are all pilgrims
headed toward home.

JUDY BLANCO & LAUREN URGENSON

Otolith

Tiny ear stone
Chronicler of time and space
A tale in rings

Day by day a life etched
Recording movement, waters, dangers, home

Center notes evoke
Rich ember yolk then mayflies, stones, caddis, midges
Signatures of ancient rock and nascent acts of living

Changing seasons leave their mark
Like the space between songs
Proof of the return or departure alone to river or sea

Thousands of miles of waves and currents in micrometers
Concentric extensions of a great journey

Each salmon gives us their story,
Their warnings, the story of the earth itself
Are we listening?

CATHERINE BULL

Salmon have translucent little bones

One for each scale, like lollipops. One for each finger, like poems. Miniature knitting needles clicking while *Jeopardy* is on. They bend like wheat in the waterlogged wind. They are flying buttresses for the color pink. They are what reading glasses for astronauts will be made of. They choke. To irridesce, to flake, to flick, to leap, and in leaping, to comb. Fast as quail legs, they xylophone. Like gills, but in multitudes. Like parentheses they plink and vibrato. They fine tooth. They seethe and sieve. They glisten and follicle. They are the workings of umbrellas, codified.

SUSAN LANDGRAF

Nugguam means to talk

Waves that never die
      talk to the salmon
      that know by smell
      their way upriver home.
Waves talk to the wind
      and the knife-sharp
      grasses that can cut
      an eye.
Wind talks with the Quinault
      where it empties
      into the sea, scours
      the clapboard siding
of the fish house. Gulls shriek
      on the roof, and the blue
      and white tsunami signs
      shake.
This is where raven
      wings shadow the mercantile
      raven who brought light
      to the Canoe and Cedar people.
This is where salmon ran
      so thick people could
      walk on water. Here
      the cedars talk
underground, bend
      listen to the wind
      to the salmon
      gulls and ravens.
This is their truth.

LINDA QUINBY LAMBERT

I Saw a Salmon Leap

From a boat on Oregon's Columbia River,
I saw a salmon leap, the slick, silvery
glint of spotted skin in an upward soar—
startling for a young girl, nine years old,
accustomed to the dry dirt and
hot asphalt of her San Joaquin Valley home.

My father put my hands on the fishing pole
so I could feel the salmon's jerk and drag
as he brought the big fish in.

Seven decades later, elderly,
but not an Elder, I learned *sche'le'ngen,*
the Salish word for *way of life,*
related to salmon, central to sustaining
the Lummi people, the Lhaq'temish Nation.

Salmon swim upstream hundreds of miles,
return home to spawn. Fishers and scientists
in my locale collect and test Chinook
from the south fork of the Nooksack,
deliver them to Skookum Hatchery
to ensure their continued strong,
stout, and brave existence.

I travel just an inch or two,
beginning, clumsy with hope,
to understand, through the prism
and prison of historical, mostly
European, definition and usage.

The word *salmon,* via Latin, *salire* (to leap)
leapt into English and crept toward

middle English, *salmoun,* and
Scottish, *salmond,* and to other tongues,
Portuguese *salmao;* Italian *sermone.*

The plainspoken Darwin noted
"male salmons fighting all day long."

Sir Walter Scott described himself
in a prone position like a "hauled salmon."

Shakespeare's Iago praised the woman who
". . . in wisdom, neuer was so fraile,
to change the Codshead for the Salmons taile."

Saint Peter, legend says, promised fisherman
bountiful catches if . . .
they did not fish on the Sabbath;
they paid their tithing in salmon.

Fishermen on the River Thames,
organized in London in 1272,
and in existence still, present a salmon
to the Dean of Westminster Abbey
every Saint Peter's Day. I admire their
longevity and their custom, this group,
The Worshipful Company of Fishmongers.

I didn't need to go so far. Nearby,
in my county, the Lummis
in their ancestral land
for thousands of years,
welcome the First Salmon
with song and ceremony,
gratitude and reverence.
The First Salmon is a sacred gift
from the storied Salmon Woman
who has sacrificed her children.
On a float of leafy branches,

uneaten parts and fish bones
are returned to the river, to be
reconstituted and continue journeying.

From a boat on Oregon's Columbia River,
the image of a big fish settled in memory.
Curiosity followed, and later, the need
for a new word: *Hy'sxwqe,* thank you
to the salmon and the people of sea and cedar.

JOANNA THOMAS

[silver] [shallow] [ripple]

sil•ver (**sil**-ver)

n. 1. sweet water, sun-flecked, flung skyward from the gush-and-rollick of plashing rapids; sparkleglint; dazzlemote. 2. a river—cold, clean, deep—sidewinding like a snake. 3. the scent of home. 4. the scent of spruce. 5. things we cannot live without: dorsal, caudal, pectoral.

shal•low (**shal**-oh)

n. 1. a place where we wait for the rain to swell the wet. 2. a placid pool, where wedded beavers feast upon alder and aspen. 3. where gravel washes back over the redd and covers the roe. 4. a scoop, a trough, a saucer; eggs and milt; eggs-an'-milt. 5. salt; sweet; milt, smolt, kelt.

rip•ple (**rip**-pel)

n. 1. here; where the stream beckons, and a fisherman fills his creel. 2. where the male stands guard while I dig a nest with my tail. 3. otoliths; ear bones; water music. 4. gill nets, fyke nets, seines, weirs. 5. my dark blue, paling to silver shot through with stars.

Fish of Knowledge

Central to it all, salmon return.
My grandpa called them "Fish of Knowledge."
They can teach things it would be good to learn,
Slip into their school as well as your college.

My grandpa called them "Fish of Knowledge."
They travel ocean as well as river.
Slip into their school as well as your college.
Show some respect to a primal giver!

They travel ocean as well as river.
They splash, rill, and spill white water and rock.
Show some respect to a primal giver!
Let them return, let the salmon restock!

They can teach things it would be good to learn.
Central to it all, salmon return.

WREN WINFIELD & RICHARD STARKEY SEAMAN

Salmon Says

Salmon says
dream with your eyes open

Salmon says
swim past the future
swim past the sea

Salmon says
this stream of thought
is heading for eternity

Salmon says
inhale
exhale
turn this white water
blue

Salmon says
forget everything
you think you know
we have no word for *end*
FIN
means on and on
we go

JULIE ROBINETT

The Genius of Salmon

Salmon, how do you know how to
travel all the way from the sea,
hundreds of miles (to exactly where you began)
with no map or directions to guide you
(aside from those written in memory,
and the earth's gentle pull)?

And what is it like to possess
a sense of scent so precise that
you can detect one drop of fragrance
in water so vast it could fill ten
Olympic-sized swimming pools?

How do you know
(you just know) how to build
a watery nest for your eggs,
without one speck
of exterior guidance?
(You get by on instinct and grace.)

Generation after generation,
you have been swept into
your beautiful dance. We humans
(and the earth, with its creatures
and plants) . . . yes, we are grateful!

LAURA DA'

Tremulousness

When a city park
lines the banks of the Sammamish

with pale trunked European beeches
to look like an English lane

beavers gnaw them to dark spears.
Black and white creatures

near the Skagit estuary
wet the eyes and blaze

the pupils with pleasure.
A dalmatian puppy levitating

from barking so hard
at harlequin ducks.

Orcas in the deep channel
of the Saratoga Passage,

preceded by a sound like an oil drum
thudding on the water. Watching

the surface of the bay the way some women stare
at a mirror as they line their eyes in black.

Trembling is a sign of infatuation
as much as debilitation

and nature is a charmer.
The quaking aspen, for example,

secreting its own form of sunscreen
as the wind hammers yellow leaves

into an embossed sheet of gold.
Salmon running the Sultan

River in a long silver link chain with
amethyst and ruby cabochon eggs.

C. R. MANLEY

Pinned

After a friend's camping trip, an emailed question
and a photo of a black rock with narrow, blue crystals,
some paired like Xs that seemed to float like fish at night.

But answering *what* and *why* depended on my asking,
Where, exactly? She dropped a pin on a map and sent the URL:
a dark, damp area at the end of a driftwood log on a gravel bar
surrounded by the North Fork of the Skykomish River.

And the story of the rock became that of the Washington coast
fifty million years ago, as subduction carried an archipelago
toward the continent in a slow motion collision.
In the doomed sea squeezed between coast and islands,
sand and mud were pushed deep enough underground
that the mineral kyanite formed in the dark mud:
narrow, blue crystals often joined in an X.

A beautiful rock. An excuse for a day trip out of town.

Halfway to Stevens Pass we turned off the pavement
and added dust to the ferns and vine maples
as the gravel road climbed a ridge and descended to the river.

Our feet in the cold water, we wobbled over slippery cobbles
to the large willow anchored in the gravel bar.
We found the driftwood log. We found the dark area

damper than expected: two inches of warm water,
stagnant but not still. As our shadows fell over it,
salmon parr four inches long wiggled over pebbles
and around the upended bodies of their brethren.

We finished the bottle of coffee, rinsed it out,
and nudged the slippery fish inside. They gazed out at us,
vertical stripes like tally marks on their sides,
tiny mouths working to keep water moving over gills.

We carried them twenty feet over the cobbles
to where the river flowed away to the west.
Upstream and down, just water and gravel bars,
with willows along the river, tall firs behind,
and beyond them the steep slopes of Spire Mountain.

We poured the fish gently into water so much cooler
and deeper than the puddle they had summered in,
and watched as they swam off into their second chance.

Then we resumed our search for beautiful rocks
with stories of how they were changed by what happened.

JORY MICKELSON

Fish School

Let the record show,
in 1958, at Fidalgo Bay,
the boats brought in
one hundred thousand salmon
per day. One million fish
in just ten. Three million
salmon a month. Such
a rain, such weather,
such a scale. The nets
& bellies of the ships
weighed down. Who
counted stack after stack
of shining forms? For ages
men have gone out
to sea, to hook, to haunt,
sweeping their nets
to bring back & bring
back & bring back. Watch
the nets burst like wet paper
sacks on the floor of the boat.

*

Are hands so different
from the paddle or a fin?
Flexing back and forth
again and again. Stretch,
expand, the muscles pushing
salmon or net through water.

*

Everything

moves—   in a wave—

the net's release, the spine
        of the salmon—   the boat—

        even the whole body
a boat rests upon.

The beating of water's
        current—   its temperature—

        even the salinity,
swell, sweeping gesture—   breath—

of the Salish Sea.

            *

When the fishing's good, the whole world
is royal—new truck
new roof—kitchen remodel.

            *

The feeding
of thousands with loaves
and fishes. The miracle
isn't in multiplication—
but the satiation
of all that hunger.

*

Sometimes, on the water, rain
swells like applause

*

I am a thief at dark's estuary,
currenting these words.

*

So many of us have spoken
about water.

Let the words fall from my mouth
like rain into the bay. One
thing the same as the other.

Let me speak into water
as a silver salmon enters
into a deep silver room.
Mercurial words into
the drapery of wave.

Let me be no more than a curtain
hung in that room beyond this door.
Word, you haven't even left my mouth
and already you are turning
as a wave folds back
and back upon itself. My words
are nothing. They've already gone
in as many ways as water says:
I hold all of this.

Water by Salmon

As life is taught by death,
and the Sun by Space,
so Clouds are taught by Land
and Rains by Place.

As Mountains are taught by Plains,
and Rivers by Lakes,
so Trees are taught by Soils,
and Elements by their Weight.

As Deserts are taught by Shores,
and Ocean Waves by Wind,
so Depth is taught by Height,
and Tides by Celestial Spin.

As Sound is taught by Silence,
and Insight by Reason,
so humans are taught by Water
and Water by Salmon.

Gratitude

Gratitude

salmonsalmonsalmEonsalmon
salmonsalmonDsalmonsalmon
salmonsalmUonsalmonsalmon
salmonsalTmonsalmonsalmon
salmonsalmoInsalmonsalmon
salmonsalmonTsalmonsalmon
salmonsalmonsalAmonsalmon
salmonsalmonsalmRonsalmon
salmonsamonsalmoGnsalmon
salmonsalmonsalmoEnsalmon
salmonsalmonsalmoDnsalmon
salmonsalmonsalmUonsalmon
salmonsalmonsalmoTnsalmon
salmonsalmonsalmoInsalmon
salmonsalmonsalmoTnsalmon
salmonsalmonsalmAonsalmon
salmonsalmonsalRmonsalmon
salmonsalmonsalGmonsalmon
salmonsalmonEsalmonsalmon
salmonsalmoDnsalmonsalmon
salmonsalmUonsalmonsalmon
salmonsalmoTnsalmonsalmon
salmonsalmIonsalmonsalmon
salmonsalmoTnsalmonsalmon
salmonsalmoAnsalmonsalmon
salmonsalmoRnsalmonsalmon
salmonsalmoGnsalmonsalmon

FOR THEM, SUCH …

My Salmon Poem

I'm looking for my poems about salmon.
I must have some around here. I'm a Native
from a fishing tribe; salmon are always near.
I am walking down the street, and salmon
in their whirling eddies swim. On my first date
I ordered the salmon, and I ate, and forgot about him.

You'd think I'd have poems about salmon,
for when poems are all that's left. American
dirt, I have a poem for that, and chrisms
that are bereft. I have a poem for the main stage
of a theater, in its largesse, a poem for the library
and a poem for this mess.

I must have a poem about salmon, the ones
that swim, the ones we eat. And of the salmon spirits
that are in images replete. Salmon are in my eye sockets,
and when I walk down the street, salmon spill out
of my pockets, salmon tap dance on fin feet.

Perhaps the absence of my poem about salmon
is as timely as the reverse. For where salmon used
to be there is now a salmon curse. And the streams
that once flowed with the salmon are backed up with
monster dams. Instead of welcoming salmon, each year
we discuss salmon programs.

Now we only dream of the salmon, we conjure them up
as though they're ghosts. We want to have them fried and
baked and dried and smoked. If I had a poem about
salmon, I'd use it just for this: to ask the salmon to

come back home, and to remove the tourniquets
that keep the salmon at bay, I'd undo what we undid.
My poem would offer the salmon a way, restore salmon to our kids.

I must have a poem about salmon.
For I am salmon culture, too.
I've got to have poems about salmon—
I didn't, but now I do.

ANDREW SHATTUCK MCBRIDE

Winter Run, Whatcom Creek

A close friend says she had a fabulous salmon dinner
prepared by her daughter's spouse. I have questions, ask,
"What kind of salmon?" She smiles. "The good kind."
      I cheer the salmon on.

I am not of this place, forego eating salmon. Others—my
sisters and brothers, and orcas—must have salmon to survive,
to renew their lives, their compact with these lands and waters.
      I too sing the salmon home.

By choice I have no permit or pole or lure.
I receive sustenance from watching the lean clocks
of salmons' bodies pushing against rushing creek waters.
      I cheer the salmon on.

Lines and color-infused lures hang entangled in trees' branches.
A beefy, youngish man with a careful blank expression
sits on a bench. His young dog, leashed, lolls nearby.
Beyond, on bloodied grass, two salmon pant.
      I sing the salmon home.

I have questions, decide finally not to ask. What do I know?
This: Along a short stretch of creek just below the noisy falls,
salmon—so close to home—swim a gauntlet. And this:
Salmon strive to live till they spawn.
      I cheer the salmon on.

KATY SHEDLOCK

Things I've Taught My East Coast Husband about Salmon

Wild is better, worth the extra cost.
None of that pale pink farmed stuff.

Their body chemistry changes.
Freshwater to ocean salt
and back. We repeated
osmoregulation every year
in science class as if
it was a spell to conjure the fish.

Atlantic salmon are extinct.

My mother always has
some salmon fillets
in the freezer the way
other people keep
ground beef.

No, it's not fishy.

No, we don't call it lox.
Yes, our bagels are terrible
but not if you don't know
what you're missing.

We should go to Issaquah sometime.
You can see the salmon come through in the fall,
hardly any fish make it
to our side of the state.

Lewis and Clark wouldn't eat them:
ten million salmon under their canoes
and they bought dogs from the tribes

for dinner. Ken Burns told us so
in eighth-grade history and the savagery
of white people shocked us
maybe for the first time.

The salmon were magic.
They leapt up Spokane Falls
like a flight of stairs.
I've never seen them
in the wild.

MOLLY BECK

Just Knowing They're Down There

Just knowing they're down there
spikes
the adrenalin, sharpens
the senses. For just a glimpse we'll perch
in the sandstone slot, alert to the slightest
movement, darkening salmon shadows.

Ever so briefly they will rest
in the cold pool
after pitting their muscle and hearts
against the impediments.

Soon
they will fan out,
fill the alluvial reaches
in a frenzy of nest building and courtship,
spume and roe,
and it's all so beautiful, this filial imperative
if only they can get there,

and they will try,
they will give it everything they've got,
they will challenge the concrete
abutments,
and where they fail,
those rivers will be lost
and our souls diminished,

but should they succeed,
the gift of effervescent recharge
prevails, and the chain
remains unbroken.

Socioeconomic

Silt muscles out the fish, gold tongues of mica
burn between gills. It's because
of flooding. It's because the schools
needed money for books so the county
let logging roar into the hills. Because
men need jobs. Our family used to eat salmon
every Thanksgiving, our plates alive with sky-
pink orange, peppered meat coating our throats.
One year, when homeless Joe
stayed for dinner, he couldn't stop exclaiming
My god this Chinook is good, so good!
As he ate, his eyes
were billowed and brown, jaw open
to what might float in. Freckles.
But mostly I recall the hands, big-wind hands,
storytelling hands, their waving like fins
treading water.

JANETTE ROSEBROOK

Coho Earn Carbon Credits

coho earn carbon credits
leave direct deposits under river stones
seep slowly into the roots of red cedar and fir
transform roe and fat into the warmth
of a brown bear's winter den.

to calculate the carbon footprint of salmon
is silly
they don't have feet.

coho are upwardly mobile,
rocketing the rapids
not earning PC points or badges
or Cascadia window decals
to wear proudly on their adipose fins
no need to calculate their carbon footprint
salmon don't need to discuss *offsets*
or *re-wilding*
are never sel-fish or meta
anything.

it is an economy of scale
milt milky swirling into a humble alchemy,
and they will transform the invisible forever,
without us

chutes and ladders
and dams
be damned.

DAYNA PATTERSON

Zombie Bears

The night is lit with the eye-shine of bears. Their jaws
make the salmon's braincase
pop. Tastiest morsel retrieved, they lumber back to the river
for more. Brains

are best. In the fish's nocturnal torpor, silver bodies bob
like logs, easy catch.
If the haul is good, only brains
will do. Headless fish litter the riverbank,

the woods. Then come, scavengers—
wolf, mink, crow. Scatter silver
scales like currency. Come, maggots and insects. Release
flesh from bone, unravel skin. Finally, you

patient trees. Rain makes a black soup,
leaching, seeping what remains
into dark roots, manifold mouths hungering for this
fathoms-deep harvest.

RICK SWANN

The Upper Reaches

I've dreamed of seeing salmon
like this—stacked up
in shallow pools
shoulder to shoulder,
dark green heads, hooked
jaws, and crimson bodies.

Unused to riparian life
they ignore my tread
along the stream's edge.
Salmon so tightly packed,
that like the bear
here before me,
I could scoop them up
and chomp them.

Why the bear moved on
with this much bounty
still to eat is a mystery
solved farther up the bank
by its scat full of huckleberries—
dessert.

CHRISTOPHER J. JARMICK

Salmon Salmon (a parody of "The Tyger")

With apologies to William Blake

Salmon, Salmon, reflecting bright,
swimming streams in our sight;
what immortal dreamed your cycle,
and blesses your journey suicidal?

In a heaven far beyond our skies,
you were muscled for jumps and glides
colored with reddish iridescent scales
taught to swim these rugged trails.

And what peoples and whose heart
will see your life beyond these parts?
And when your gills take first breath
Do you feel your future death?

How are you born in freshwater
able to live in salt and grow bigger, stronger?
Eat insects, get key species title
become food for bears, so environmentally vital.

When you shift with the season
do you question the reason?
Or celebrate your cycle with glee?
Did the one who made man also make thee?

Salmon, Salmon, reflecting bright,
swimming streams in our sight;
what immortal dreamed your cycle,
and blesses your journey suicidal?

NEIL MCKAY

The Salmyn

After William Blake

Salmyn, Salmyn, quick and quiver,
To the sea and back up river,
What immortal chromosome
Could weave thy will to return home?

On what shores of paradise
Did thou first give sacrifice?
And when they saw your magnitude,
What hands were raised in gratitude?

What consecration, what secret prayer
Called you to the fisher's snare?
What amnesty, what state of grace,
Could bring you to this holy place?

And what shoulder, and what net,
Could twist you like a marionette?
And when thy heart did end its beat,
What calloused hand, what steady feet?

When you stopped your slap and thresh,
And fed the children with your flesh,
Did they smile, your gift receive?
Did they who tasted Lamb taste thee?

Salmyn, Salmyn, quick and quiver,
To the sea and back up river,
What immortal chromosome
Could weave thy will to return home?

JOAN ROGER

Cento for the Salmon

So early it's still almost dark out
A wind from the pine-trees trickles on my bare head
I am just a shadow
In the eddies of the water
And I am ready like the young salmon

In shade, beneath hidden stars
At the source of the longest river
The birds have quieted in the forest
And I lift them
And that too is more than enough

If only I could look beneath my skin
As if death were nowhere
Feel the future dissolve in a moment
Into a stream, an arc of water
This is a special way of being afraid

Go back into your mist
Beyond this place of wrath and tears
Past the strip malls and the power plants
Past the near meadow, over the still stream
Open your eyes to water

It is still a beautiful world
Even when I am no one
Remember the sky that you were born under
At the ragged edge of the tree line, sheltered by conifer and bay
It is time for us to wake

For too many nights now I have not imagined the salmon
We had been together so very long
The course of the river changed

But that did not keep me from crossing
I begin again with the smallest numbers

To start. That's everything we require to keep going
To learn the song the first one laid down
I heard it in the streets, I heard it
And again, in some shadowy future
None of us will ever know

Examine all you have
All the unintended wounds
And treat those two imposters just the same
Ask for forgiveness
Then we can find our way

The time will come
To reteach a thing its loveliness
No less than the trees and the stars
When the soul lies down in that grass
What can anyone give you greater than now

And the point is, to live everything
For there are so many ways
We stand at the prow again of a small ship
No other shore, only this bank
I reached to love them all

There are a hundred ways to kneel and kiss the ground
But here alone
Save your strength to swim with the tide
Say only, thank you
I will love you again

MADELINE SWEET

Nature's Candy

a salmon wrapped in tinfoil
holds all his words
toes of all sorts make their way to the yard
slowly the fisherman uncoils his catch
I offer up my thin hands for a taste
nature's candy
he calls it
filling gaps in mind and spirit
extending a care and a word cloaked in flavor
stories picked out in fish bones
nature's candy
caught from the silent line of the fisherman
even the dogs share in our feast
tails wagging
mouths glistening

KATY E. ELLIS

The Ones Who Walk Again

A Duwamish man told the story
in my daughter's grade school assembly.
He drummed open a world
of children who walk into the water
and who return as Salmon
for the villagers to eat.

Now she worries beyond reason
for the Salmon boys and Salmon girls—
the ones who will not walk again
should the drying bones of our last-night's dinner
not be returned to sea.

Always the ocean down our street
keeps up its chop and spit and rush
and I sack lunches, pay bills, wash clothes
in cycles spinning my hand-me-down stories,
the ones I will not give her.

She plucks each bone of a heart-held story
from the dish in her hands
and feeds them to the waves that slosh
against her legs growing sturdy
as the underpinnings of a miles-long pier.

JOANNE M. CLARKSON

Salmon Bones

for Judy DuPuis, Chehalis

She is speaking for the stream, storyteller
dressed in her cedar skirt, her braid ribboned
by silver riffles like the river. Children
in the park listen, parents beside them.
People passing are drawn close by a voice
belonging to water. It is a hunger song:
When the fields were barren, the People
cried out to Creator, promising, if food
were given, to return a portion to nourish
the future. Creator heard the plea
and spread his might across the oceans.
So many fish filled the streams, they
leaped with salmon, flowing backwards.
The People caught the shining creatures
with their fingers. Had a feast. Then gathered
every single bone, from the flexible backbone
to the tiny needles of ribs. In gratitude,
they floated them back into the rivers.
In season, these grew into more fish
even as the People grew in body and wisdom
so that the salmon and the People and the stream
became One.

EILEYAH AHMAD
FIRST GRADE

We Are Salmon People

Bears, Birds, Seals, Bass, Eagles, and People
All eat this create, salmon gives all life
Salmon gives us nutrients, vitamins, and riches
They live in water, fresh, and salt water

A Native story tells us
When you eat salmon, you must return the bones to the water
To respect the Salmon people
What you do in the land, affects the things in the water

Egg, alevin, fry, parr, smolt, adult, and death
Everything in the life of the salmon is a cycle
Baby, child, teenager, adult, old, and death
Everything in the life of human is a cycle
The world is part of a cycle, we are Salmon people

GAIL TREMBLAY

Comparing Sockeye and King Salmon

It starts as soon as you get the fish home—
take it out of the bag and start to prepare it to cook.
The sockeye has a darker coral color, flesh
more beautiful than the petals of the quince flowers
whose floral elegance ushers in the spring—
one wonders what can make this thin slab of muscle
so bright the color almost quivers in the hand.
And when one turns the fish over, the skin glints,
a lively silver side against a blue-black back
that seems to make the silver glitter in the sun.
This slab of salmon gives you pleasure
before you even get it in the pan.
Next to sockeye, a piece of king is thick and pale.
The color is gentle like pink beads
of angel skin coral or the flowers of a rare
coral peony whose petals fade to a delicate creamy
color that blends pink and pale orange
in a way difficult to describe. The skin of king
is also paler, the broad belly iridescent white,
the side a less scintillating silver, the back
more ordinary shades of black and charcoal gray.
But the weight of this big slab of fish is pleasing
in the hand. One feels the greater distance
that this swimmer traveled, the magic
that allowed him to grow to such a size.
The cooking is a delicate affair—king goes
into the oven longer; thin sockeye for less
than fifteen minutes or it's dry. One checks
early, impatient for the moment when the flesh
is moist but cooked enough so the layers of fish
will separate easily, revealing the row of long,
fine bones that one stacks on the edge of the plate
before slipping the tender piece of fish

between the teeth. This moment is pure chemistry—
the instant pleasure that makes eating art
instead of merely feeding the gut. The tongue
searches for subtle differences. What is it
beside color that separates the sockeye from the king?
The sockeye has a slightly finer grain; fish melts
inside your mouth and oils create a delicate bouquet
that titillates the taste buds so each bite slips
down the throat, a pungent pleasure one longs
to repeat. But, oh, the king is slightly sweeter,
layers thicker, the grain so startlingly smooth—
each bite has a succulence that makes sense.
Celebrate the difference. In the end, it's all desire.

FINN COFFIN

Recurring Advice to Myself

Oily pink flesh
Flakes off in zigzags
White wine sauce
With lemon and shallots
And butter, lots of butter
A bone pokes your cheek
Store-bought salmon
Filleted without care
By some pimply kid
They always miss pin bones
Next time, calm down
Go to the indigenous place
A low shack with fresh fish
Once by the river
Now in a parking lot
Next to a wind-sports store
Where all the bones are plucked
Lose the fancy flavors
Try this instead
Half a lemon, brown sugar
Maybe some fresh dill

KAREN BONAUDI

Escape

He swam in the dill butter sauce
on the porcelain plate spattering
the silk and linened guests, some shocked
some amused, some raising their knives.
He leapt to a bowl of bouillabaisse
at another diner's table, felt rich broth
coat his mouth and gills.
His fish brain knew this was not
how he wanted to die.
He flew higher, out the door
into the street where a rain puddle
sent him through a gutter, a culvert
to a retention pond where he was larger
than the ducks that bid him au revoir
as he took to the sky, became a cloud,
fish scales forecasting rain,
floating with other hungered searchers
on westerlies in their own
atmospheric river that flows
as long as the earth.

SUSAN RICH

Food for Fallen Angels

If food be the music of love, play on

Twelfth Night, misremembered

If they can remember living at all, it is the food they miss:
a plate of goji berries, pickled ginger, a pink salmon
dressed on a bed of miniature thyme, a spoon

glistening with pomegranate seeds, Russian black bread
lavished with July cherries so sweet, it was dangerous to revive;
to slide slowly above the lips, flick and swallow—almost, but not quite.

Perhaps more like this summer night: cohos in the lemon grove—
a picnicker's trick of moonlight and platters; the table dressed
in gold kissed glass, napkins spread smooth as dark chocolate.

If they sample a pastry—glazed Florentine, praline hearts—
heaven is lost. It's the cinnamon and salt our souls return for—
lux on the tongue, the clove of garlic: fresh and flirtatious.

NANCY PAGH

Spring Salmon at Night

I thought the west wind called me from bed
the night the river ran so hard.
I followed it over the moonlit lawn
across the road and into the woods,
climbing fallen cedars and moving
beyond the skunk cabbages. I followed
the west wind to the riverbed and
plunged my legs in dark water
that sucked and swirled behind my knees
and tried to pull me beyond the bank.

And the wind stopped.
And I forgot why I came out in the night.
And I clenched the underwater moss with my toes
and was lost
until the spring salmon came,
their torpedo-shaped bodies knowing me
as another follower of currents.
In the cold gray river the spring salmon
found and circled me, their forms almost warm
as they touched the backs of my legs
guiding me back through the forest
across suburban lawns and down my own hallway
from bedroom to kitchen
until I found myself standing at the cat-food cupboard
and recognized each cat circling my legs
and my own gullibility
or desire to be led
in the direction of someone else's hunger.

RAYMOND CARVER

At Night the Salmon Move

At night the salmon move
out from the river and into town.
They avoid places with names
like Foster's Freeze, A & W, Smiley's,
but swim close to the tract
homes on Wright Avenue where sometimes
in the early morning hours
you can hear them trying doorknobs
or bumping against Cable TV lines.
We wait up for them.
We leave our back windows open
and call out when we hear a splash.
Mornings are a disappointment.

APRIL RYAN

Midnight Market Window

Oh, I remember fifty years ago
disappointment, CLOSED sign.
Nightlight on the blackboard,
words written in pinkish chalk:
salmon cheeks—salmon rolls—
smoked salmon—salmon jerky—
salmon on a stick—salmon fillet—
crispy skin—cedar-plank salmon.
Fresh caught salmon ready to
bake, grill, roast, or panfry.
Tonight's specialty: BBQ Fish Lips.
I still wonder, joke or one last kiss?

LINERA LUCAS

Where was the best salmon of my life?

In Port Chilkoot, forty years ago, we caught a run of Chinook.
I was recently divorced and had flown to old friends in Alaska to be cosseted.
There is very little cosseting on a fishing boat, or in a fishing family,
but they let me come out on the gillnetter with them, and later
they let me eat as much smoked salmon as I wanted. As much as I wanted
was not something I had in my marriage,
although I had enough divorce.

When I say we *caught the fish*,
my job was to stay out of the way.
Out of the way of the roller winding up the net full of shining fish,
out of the way as my friends released the waterfall of fish into the ice hold,
slowly enough for two of them to double-gaff a big Chinook,
hang the fish by its gills and get its weight—forty pounds—
then we powered back to port.

I was allowed to gut the fish and pull out its entrails.
I didn't read the entrails like a diviner, and I regret this.
At the time I wanted to get the guts out of something. A dead fish was good enough.
When the flesh was clean and the smoker ready,
the salmon went inside to have a hot hibernation.
We ate the salmon with lemon. I remember also cabbage slaw, homemade pickles,
cinnamon buttermilk pie for dessert.

We ate the tender flesh still warm from the smoker,
and I loved that salmon as I have never loved another salmon,
wild, fresh, hot, almost melting,
as if I had ascended into salmon heaven.
No bread or onion or dill—
just the tart lemon and the salmon caught by my friends,
and I was filled.

KATHLEEN FLENNIKEN

My Salmon

I was ten when I hooked him.
My dad and the skipper rushed over
and we reeled in the biggest catch of the day.
I struggled to hold him aloft for a photo
I've since lost and my fellow fishermen joked
that my salmon and I were twins.

My mother roasted him over coals
on an Oregon beach. I remember
the evening lit in perpetual pink
and taking full credit for feeding my family
and our new fishing-boat friends.

It was my salmon who fed us.
My salmon, who kept swimming
deeper and further, still hooked to my line,
dodging whatever it is that makes me forget
most of the days of my life.

I'll never again try to haul him up.
It's more like I'm holding him in my sights
in an ocean as pink as a sky at dusk.
Pink as his flesh.
I remember his flesh, his unzipped spine.

Sometimes he surfaces,
nudging the liminal space between
but I'm never sure between what and what—
myself and forgiveness, earth and death?

I can't make it out. Then he goes back
to the depths, a silver and rainbow flash
in the current behind my eyes.

GABRIELLE BATES

Salmon

My father and I sit at a sushi bar in my new city
sampling three different kinds of salmon nigiri.

He tells me about a great funeral speech
he recently heard a son give for his father.

The speech was structured around regrets
everyone assumed the father didn't have,

interspersed with hilarious stories involving boys
crashing the family van and fishing mishaps.

The ivory salmon is pale and impossibly soft.
The sliver of steelhead, orange enough

to pretend it's salmon. How else to say it.
I am my father's only child, and he is my mother.

We dip our chopsticks into a horseradish paste
dyed green and called wasabi. I know his regrets.

I could list them. But instead at his funeral
I will talk, if I can talk, about nights like this,

how good it felt just to be next to him,
to be the closest thing he had.

SYLVIA BYRNE POLLACK

A Salmon Scale Is Called a Cycloid

The first salmon I met had no silvered scales.
Sheathed in a tin can, it was liberated by my mother
with a hand-cranked can opener. She mixed
the orange flesh with egg and cracker crumbs,
fried patties for our supper. Decades later,
when I moved from the East Coast to
the Pacific Northwest, I was shocked to see
fresh caught salmon, cheaper than hamburger!

I marveled at heaped, no longer leaping,
glistening bodies, piled on ice at Pike Place Market.
I learned to prepare this fish and now, despite its
beef-eclipsing price, serve it at least once a week.
So delicious, but never as good as salmon roasted
over an open fire on an alder plank, served with
salads and fry bread to celebrate Vi Hilbert's
birthday each July. Memories of those feasts
reverberate, wind chime made of salmon scales.

SUSAN CHASE-FOSTER

Sin of Omission

There was a salmon leaping
across the red paper label
on the tin can our mom pried open
to avoid cooking meat,
a culinary sin on Fridays.
We loved the pink flesh,
the tiny bones
bubbled with buttered flour,
a drizzle of milk,
spooned on toast
and topped with a lemon slice
translucent as stained glass.

Bless us O Lord and these Thy gifts
which we are about to devour!
my brothers blurted out,
pounded the table,
fell off their chairs choking
on their own silliness
while I, big sister,
wannabe saint
trembling with solemnity,
remained silent,
tried not to smile,
though our mom did at me.

There was a salmon on my plate
who I failed to thank,
surely a greater sin
than eating meat on Friday,
but I never thought of her or him
as a real salmon or even a fish,
a swimming, breathing,

finning, leaping, sentient being,
like those tilapia I heard
Jesus multiplied
on the Sea of Galilee.

Until one Friday in second grade
a kid at lunch chanted
Salmon, salmon, always salmon!
igniting Sister Ignacia—
an explosion of nun in a black habit
and white-finned cornette—
into shaming the kid
and the rest of us
with her saltwater tears
of appreciation for the salmon
she was currently consuming,
the salmon who died
after fin-grinding up a raging river,
laying a thousand eggs,
some to become the hooked or netted,
dried, fried, filleted, or canned
like the salmon we second graders
were eating right this minute
to stay alive, and free
from the transgression of stuffing cows
and chickens and pigs, for God's sake,
into our tiny mouths just one day a week,
five weeks max a month,
fifty-two days a year.
Is that too much to ask?

Parched of tears and words
Sister Ignacia raised a forkful of salmon
with her two hands like a priest
consecrating a host.
Thank you, Salmon, she whispered
and held that holy offering so Heaven-high
that she levitated clear up to the ceiling

until some of the more saintly among us
shouted *Amen!* and she dropped
like a feather
back down to the floor again.

The Curved Shape of Salmon Mouths

Do not forgive us this trespass
the scent of field-dressed salmon lost on a breeze
replaced by something called a *fish taxi, fish ladder,*
fish farm, aquaculture,
the apex of the rise of man, teach children of
the valleys to count all five varieties of salmon
on fingers even if
you cannot see them
in the rivers

I wish for the salmon to return
run thick in the rivers, in bays,
to have old men tell tall tales
say they've never seen 'em so thick
you can set your watch by them,
and your seasons

A man says you can walk on them
from island to island without getting wet
and the woman says you could find you a lover
by crossing the seas on the backs of salmon

And all the people give thanks
lift hands in ceremony, build beach fire
and fat on the bones from pinks, cohos,
Chinooks is a wholeness on the cover
of magazines, not
an echo
mother to daughter
one person turning face to another
saying, here take me, all of me

In deep heart, the dance of two hands
moving cosmos, the soul vibration
of the universe in expansion,
the pull of a braided silk line to shore
filled with glittering beach stone,
a salmon flopping in wet sand
with a minnow in its mouth.

Choices

SCOTT BENTLEY

The sʔuladxʷ Map of Seattle

sʔuladxʷ sʔuladxʷ sʔuladxʷ sʔuladxʷ
sʔuladxʷ sʔula x sʔuladxʷ sʔuladxʷ
sʔuladxʷ sʔuladxʷ sʔuladxʷ sʔuladxʷ
sʔuladxʷ sʔuladxʷ sʔuladxʷ sʔuladxʷ
sʔuladxʷ Salmon Salmon Salmon sʔuladxʷ
sʔuladxʷ Salmon Salmon Salmon Salmon
sʔuladxʷ Salmon Salmon Salmon Salmon
sʔuladxʷ Salmon Salmon Salmon Salmon sʔuladxʷ
sʔuladxʷ Salmon Salmon Salmon Salmon sʔuladxʷ
sʔuladxʷ Salmon sʔuladxʷ Salmon Salmon sʔuladxʷ
sʔuladxʷ Salmon sʔuladxʷ Salmon Salmon Salmon sʔuladxʷ
sʔuladxʷ Salmon sʔuladxʷ Salmon Salmon Salmon Salmon
Salmon Salmon Salmon Salmon Salmon Salmon
sʔuladxʷ Salmon Salmon Salmon Salmon sʔuladxʷ
sʔuladxʷ Salmon Salmon Salmon sʔuladxʷ sʔuladxʷ
sʔuladxʷ Salmon Salmon Salmon Salmon sʔuladxʷ
sʔuladxʷ Salmon Salmon Salmon Salmon
sʔuladxʷ Salmon sʔuladxʷ Salmon Salmon sʔuladxʷ
sʔuladxʷ Salmon Salmon Salmon sʔuladxʷ
Salmon Salmon Salmon Salmon
sʔuladxʷ Salmon Salmon Salmon
Salmon Salmon Salmon sʔuladxʷ
sʔuladxʷ Salmon sʔuladxʷ sʔuladxʷ
Salmon Salmon
Salmon Salmon
sʔuladxʷ sʔuladxʷ
Salmon
sʔuladxʷ sʔuladxʷ
Salmon
Salmon Salmon Salmon Salmon
Salmon Salmon Salmon Salmon Salmon
Salmon Salmon Salmon Salmon Salmon sʔuladxʷ
sʔuladx Salmon Salmon Salmon Salmon Salmon
Salmon Salmon Salmon Salmon Salmon Salmon
sʔuladxʷ Salmon Salmon Salmon Salmon Salmon Salmon
sʔuladxʷ Salmon Salmon Salmon Salmon Salmon
sʔuladxʷ Salmon Salmon Salmon Salmon sʔuladxʷ
sʔuladxʷ Salmon sʔuladxʷ Salmon sʔuladxʷ sʔuladxʷ
sʔuladxʷ sʔuladxʷ Salmon Salmon Salmon sʔuladxʷ
sʔuladxʷ Salmon sʔuladxʷ Salmon Salmon
Salmon Salmon sʔuladxʷ Salmon
sʔuladxʷ sʔuladxʷ sʔuladxʷ Salmon
sʔuladxʷ Salmon sʔuladxʷ sʔuladxʷ sʔuladxʷ Salmon
sʔuladxʷ sʔuladxʷ sʔuladxʷ sʔuladxʷ Salmon
sʔuladxʷ sʔuladxʷ
sʔuladxʷ
sʔuladxʷ
sʔuladxʷ

CATHERINE CRAWFORD

Ho' oponopono to the salmon

. . . an apology

I am sorry
 your path home has been blocked by cities greedy for water
 for the waste of your life killed in the turbines of dams
 for not reaching out to nations that need you to survive
 for how I've seen "nation" as something big and important.

Please forgive me
 for the plastic that reaches your sea in spite of recycling
 for not saying "thank you" when I've taken you into my body
 for walking the land we share and leaving a giant footprint
 for all forms of denial I'm still blind to.

Thank you
 for your brothers who sleep in my freezer
 for their gift of mineral wealth from the ocean
 for reminding me wasting food is a sin of privilege
 for feeding the world with the light of your leaping.

I love you
 for your patience to wait till it's time to start a journey
 for refusing to bow to barriers that suck breath from your body
 for feeding foxes, bears, and people I've let slip under my radar
 for launching yourself without fear into a future of fertile darkness.

JIM BERTOLINO

Salmon Breathing

The Skagit Valley breathes
salmon: the in-breath

when salmon swim up
the Skagit River to spawn.

Then the streams cough
as dying salmon clog the shallows.

I love the easing out-breath
as hatchlings swim to the sea.

This cycle of the valley breathing salmon
has continued for thousands

of seasons but has become irregular
and weak. I fear soon

there will be no salmon
bringing breath to the valley.

RONDA PISZK BROATCH

Sometimes, I Tell the Universe

This is how events will unfold: the eagle
will catch the salmon, or the salmon will live another day
nearer to spawning, evolve as sustenance

for resident orcas who are diminishing
in astonishing numbers. Sometimes I tell the Universe
that I, being a part of every living thing,

declare an equal say,
and that I say no, I will not succumb
to exploitation, become a statistic

on the planet's list of casualties,
not lose my life my dears my loves
to extinction or the mutterings of deniers, that hope

is a choice I make, that somehow—and by this I mean
I will it so—the waters will cool a little, the salmon will
thread their way, creating redds in all the rivers, orca young

grow to mate to flourish to teach us their wisdom
before time stretches its elastic to exhaustion.
Sometimes *rise* doesn't have to mean

sea level, but rather rebellion and compassion, mean
stitching rescue to our breast pockets, weaving time
into lifelines to each wild and fragile body.

SHANKAR NARAYAN

Salmon Circle the RAS Tank until Reaching Market Weight

Farming salmon is the moral equivalent to farming hawks.

Becca Franks, New York University

1

This is the miracle.   This body,

itself containing unfathomable
pull of planet and birthplace, unnamable
because words in which this wonder
lived, which could tease apart the iridescent
infinite in every scale, name differently salt
from sweet, subjugated from survivor, are genocided to whisper, leaving us
colonizer tongue, every vein and bone
commodity, and to call this body
limber or lithe or quicksilver would be to succumb
to assimilation, which is scarcity
of imagination, which is what
colonization is—leaving us again
without words, only bodies translating into flesh
the magnet of sky, bodies born to go home or die,
fight the fight of this planet
before us. All within
this miracle. This miracle
circling and circling

2

our cage.   This is the miracle—this panopticon,

this Recirculating Aquaculture System, this end state
of our evolution, this sky-eating drum
too small to satisfy endless hunger, this nature

humanized, bodies packed in, no inch wasted,
currents to swim against our artifice, white
lights so bright their eyes evolve smaller with each generation, waste
flushed into river, salinity calibrated
to life-stage, perfect as bodies who journey only
to the same single riverbed to die, because we too demand perfection
in our prey, demand nothing less than perfect
bodies to consume, feed deconstructed fish to other fish
because they were the wrong fish for our perfect tongues.   They kept escaping
so we hardened the cage as we have practiced
for centuries to do, and now behold the miracle—
the hawk grounded, the lion tamed and farmed. This miracle,
mirror-world in oily sheen, our image

3

in bionic irises. The miracle is not fish

that shrinks ocean, not tank that magics
meat machine, none of these but the algorithm that perfects
this system, choreographs this dance, creates
the optimal cell, mimics current so real we believe the fish believe
as they circle and circle, as we believe in the algorithm
that deifies the data doubles of us, and each fish too has a data
double that circles and circles its digital tank, where nothing
cannot be known, where the algorithm makes no small mistakes, just exponentializes
till detonation, till intelligence overrides intelligence
of fish's body, overrides our own body, override, override, override
as data doubles surrender, stare into fluorescence so bedazzling they forget
the data double of a planet is not itself a planet, forget
that we too once had bodies, bodies
with lungs and guts pulsing capillaries with blood and heme that feels
a burning core, whose fins and tails propelled us up-
river to become bloody bodies birthing and feeding
grizzlies below unending blue glaciers, bodies, bodies, bodies

4

that lived.	Bodies
that served.	Bodies
fit for the end.	Were we not ourselves
such perfect miracles?	Were we not born
to fight the drowning	cascade? Does our body
not recollect	each multicolored pebble
in that one perfect	riverbed? How our mother gave
her body so we could become	self? And what was coded
into each real cell	of our real bodies
which will never	be doubled? Coded
into blood	clear as river. Scatter our flesh
into water of home.	Overwrite. Override. Survive.

PETER DONALDSON

from "Salmon Circle Symphony"

5. Downstream

Freshet floods release! Freshet spring!
Freshet rise and let me ride
downstream, down canyon, cascade and valley wide
as in my dream.

Memorize these.

Odor of alderwood,
fragrance of sandstone,
scent of gleaming glacier,
granite's face a pebbled fate,
slide of slate and old basalt,
perfume of beaver dam, rank of iron,
scant sketch of sulfur skunk cabbage soliloquies,
bouquets of moss, fallen log,
vocal fumes from a raccoon bog,
confluence thirteen, fourteen,
rapid voices rejoice cascading
gravity's laziest choices,
open wide mayfly eyes,
the valley meandering we ride
past railroad ties, timber buys,
reservoir backwater, slack-water, black-water,
warnings, warmer,
time lost is time mistrusted,
anchored aroma creosote encrusted,
concrete backdrop, log boom blunder, pulled asunder,
blunder, blunder! turbines thunder! bubbles
rumble, spill gate tumbles upside downstream me
mixed, nitrogen fixed, raceway, race
away alder beach to picnic reach,

farm to fields, fecund yields bovine pee,
wink of dairy, fertilizer spree, whiff, sniff of industry,
stinking zinc of galvanized culvert,
sentient impasse, chemical morass
swiftly move me, swiftly past
marina pilings, rainbow spills,
petrol, diesel, aching gills,
profane asphalt introductions,
impervious sensory deconstructions,
copper, mercury, crank case oil drop,
overflow, storm drain, dog crap runoff,
vociferous, olfactory, aquatic malaprop, O malodorous
big blind river,
remember me, please, all of these . . .

backwards.

DEIRDRE LOCKWOOD

Three Salmon Redactions

redact: from Latin redigere: *"to bring back" or "to reduce"*

1. Mortal

In U.S. Pacific Northwest coho salmon (*Oncorhynchus kisutch*), stormwater exposure annually causes unexplained acute mortality when adult salmon migrate to urban creeks to reproduce. By investigating this phenomenon, we identified a highly toxic quinone transformation product of N-(1,3-dimethylbutyl)-N'-phenyl-p-phenylenediamine (6PPD), a globally ubiquitous tire rubber antioxidant. Retrospective analysis of representative roadway runoff and stormwater-affected creeks of the U.S. West Coast indicated widespread occurrence of 6PPD-quinone (<0.3 to 19 micrograms per liter) at toxic concentrations (median lethal concentration of 0.8 ± 0.16 micrograms per liter). These results reveal unanticipated risks of 6PPD antioxidants to an aquatic species and imply toxicological relevance for dissipated tire rubber residues.

2. Home scent

Elevated concentrations of CO_2 in seawater can disrupt numerous sensory systems in marine fish. This is of particular concern for Pacific salmon because they rely on olfaction during all aspects of their life including during their homing migrations from the ocean back to their natal streams. We investigated the effects of elevated seawater CO_2 on coho salmon (*Oncorhynchus kisutch*) olfactory-mediated behavior, neural signaling, and gene expression within the peripheral and central olfactory system. Ocean-phase coho salmon were exposed to three levels of CO_2, ranging from those currently found in ambient marine water to projected future levels. Juvenile coho salmon exposed to elevated CO_2 levels for 2 weeks no longer avoided a skin extract odor that elicited avoidance responses in coho salmon maintained in ambient CO_2 seawater. Exposure to these elevated CO_2 levels did not alter odor signaling in the olfactory epithelium, but did induce significant changes in signaling within the olfactory bulb. RNA-Seq analysis of olfactory tissues revealed extensive disruption in expression of genes involved in neuronal signaling within the olfactory bulb of salmon exposed to elevated CO_2, with lesser impacts on gene expression in the olfactory rosettes. The disruption in olfactory bulb gene pathways included genes associated with GABA signaling and maintenance of ion balance within bulbar neurons. Our results indicate that ocean-phase coho salmon exposed to elevated CO_2 can experience significant behavioral impairments likely driven by alteration in higher-order neural signal processing within the olfactory bulb. Our study demonstrates that anadromous fish such as salmon may share a sensitivity to rising CO_2 levels with obligate marine species suggesting a more wide-scale ecological impact of ocean acidification.

3. Elwha

The removal of two large dams on the Elwha River was completed in 2014 with a goal of restoring anadromous salmonid populations. Using observations from ongoing field studies, we compiled a timeline of migratory fish passage upstream of each dam. We also used spatially continuous snorkeling surveys in consecutive years before (2007, 2008) and after (2018, 2019) dam removal during summer baseflow to assess changes in fish distribution and density over 65 km of the mainstem Elwha River. Before dam removal, anadromous fishes were limited to the 7.9 km section of river downstream of Elwha Dam, potamodromous species could not migrate throughout the river system, and resident trout were the most abundant species. After dam removal, there was rapid passage into areas upstream of Elwha Dam, with 8 anadromous species (Chinook, Coho, Sockeye, Pink, Chum, Winter Steelhead, Summer Steelhead, Pacific Lamprey, and Bull Trout) observed within 2.5 years. All of these runs except Chum Salmon were also observed in upper Elwha upstream of Glines Canyon Dam within 5 years. The spatial extent of fish passage by adult Chinook Salmon and Summer Steelhead increased by 50 km and 60 km, respectively, after dam removal. Adult Chinook Salmon densities in some previously inaccessible reaches in the middle section of the river exceeded the highest densities observed in the lower section of the river prior to dam removal. The large number (>100) of adult Summer Steelhead in the upper river after dam removal was notable because it was among the rarest anadromous species in the Elwha River prior to dam removal. The spatial extent of trout and Bull Trout remained unchanged after dam removal, but their total abundance increased and their highest densities shifted from the lower 25 km of the river to the upper 40 km. Our results show that reconnecting the Elwha River through dam removal provided fish access to portions of the watershed that had been blocked for nearly a century.

MITZI MCMILLAN MOORE

Extinct

Summer 2016

What would we call a species that
forgot how to fly like a flock

of birds,
or how to feed their babies,

how to swim like a school of salmon,
or how to school their young,

how to create a home
like a hive of honey bees,

or how to care for their Queen,
Mother Earth?

JULENE TRIPP WEAVER

Salmon: Our Northwest Pride

Restaurants in the great Northwest, proud
to have salmon on their menu, grilled or baked
or pan fried with a sauce and lemon on the side.
Rich in omega-3, fresh pink to red flesh:
the coho, the Chinook, seasonal, named
after a river, after a Native tribe.

At the Ballard Locks I learn about their long
journey, how we've interrupted their lives
with our dams and infiltration, how devoted
we are to correction, these locks exemplar.
We offer land acknowledgments at poetry
readings and socially conscious events.

Their lives in danger, we the mode
of extinction destroy estuaries. Tourists
buy smoked salmon at a state gift shop,
or find it fresh off a boat from Natives
who embody mutual respect
for these ancient creatures, their renewal

each year a celebration of life.
We've much to learn to change our ways,
to appreciate, to restore a world where salmon
thrive. We've contaminated them with our
debris, our chemicals—ingested when we gorge
on our Northwest pride.

BRAD MONSMA

Pipestream

Data on Longfellow Creek

Pacific Terminals
Puget Sound Freight Lines
Terminal 5 train tracks
W. Marginal Way
Vane Brothers shipping company
Nucor Steel,
old cars and broken trailers
lined up in October rain.
Things coho leaving the sound pass beneath,
improbable as dreams.

The grated pipe receives the creek you transect.
You walk upstream, sometimes with those who emerge
to throw last life at the beaver dam.

Waiting, wading, angling for purchase on the mud banks,
tangled in beaver-felled maples and alders, you rethink,
double back for a clear path.

In the pool beyond the sluice rest three bodies,
pinks and skies and seas, stippled green.
You reach in for the gray-lost saturation.

You measure sudden death, note the wild adipose fin.
Cutting in, you fold back the belly with careful cold fingers.
All the red in the world spills onto the sand,
pearls worth everything and nothing.

Yet today, three coho dance a new redd, each twist
each opening gill racing 6PPD-quinone
from your car tires flowing deep into their every fiber.

Rain starts again. Upstream from the pipe,
Tom will dip a camera into a pool and see a
shadow of new life finning under the cut bank.

Downstream:
blue tarps on trailers next to rusty gas grills
   yellow dump trucks and muddy payloaders
        piles of mangled rebar
            tracks laid on sleepers
                boxes addressed and waiting
                    ships heading out to sea.

DARREN NORDLIE

Reflections on Fishing Chinook with My Uncle

My uncle taught me how to cast a rod,
a mighty tug almost pulled me,
he grabbed my handle from behind and
together we reeled in a silvery, black-spotted Chinook.
Its fins sparkled in the sun as a million foam bubbles.
He told me if we take care of this
stream, it will take care of us.

Now I leave my line in for a whole day
and leave home empty-handed.
Looking at photos of me and
my uncle holding shiny salmon,
I couldn't bear to see his face and tell him
there are no Chinook in the stream anymore.

ALEXANDER A. MANZONI

May You Leap Upstream

So numerous were they—*once*.
　　So numerous, before the tide of industrialized humanity thus deplet'd the stocks.
　　　'Tis a tide that has not yet retreat'd.

Salmon, O salmon.
You nourish the bears, and in turn, the forests.
Your bodies, so in tune with the environment, require specific temperatures with
　　　　　　　which to thrive and breed.
Did the white man really need to take it this far—and for so long?
Even after they figured out it was wrong—the environmental destruction continues.

Salmon. O salmon.
　　Spotted. King. Atlantic. Sockeye.
　　　One cannot reasonably deny the impact you've had on this world.
　　　But now? Your existence is in peril.
　　　Many of your kin, they are being farmed, harvested,
　　　　　　as if fish are the same as a crop of soybeans.
They. Are. Not.

So, what to do?
The capitalist CEOs want to pass this over onto you.
Instead of them doing anything to assuage the damage they cause/have caused,
　　they expect us to
　　go without—to make big changes in our lives
　　whilst still acting like they are being "eco-friendly" and all.

　　　The ivory tower, it stands formidable, looming tall o'er the distraught denizens.
　　A little man with big plans—atop the penthouse floor, he decides the course
　　　　　of many.
You care naught for the well-being of the Earth, the well-being of all the creatures that
　　　　　continue to exist upon it.

O salmon. With your inward strength, may you leap upstream, o'er the dashing rocks.
May you *leap* against the current, right through the plate-glass
windows, and *into* Mr. Ivory Tower's palatial office.
May you fill his expensive luxury items with the rank smell of angered ichthyoids.
And may the sun align most properly.

> To teach him a lesson about salmon.
> One he shall not soon forget.

JERRY BRYAN

A Columbia River Dam's Confession to the Salmon

I serve colonialist men. I flood Indigenous lands and waterfalls.
I kill First Foods; conscripted slave, I am; concrete controlled
at the cold command of white supremacist man. I slaughter
salmon, like the butchering of plains buffalos. I am that
       instrument of cultural genocide.
I starve orcas; kill Indigenous peoples. I am the wealth of kings,
like Shelley's Ozymandias: "Look on my Works, ye Mighty,
       and despair!"
You salmon shall not pass this way again. I make my koi ponds
Hot, wrap you in toxic algae; I poach you on your way to the sea.
My frenzied water, my machines' screams—I kill you coming home.
       No one can hear you cry.
I am white man's headsman, doing my sadistic job, my fish
       ladders the selection ramps of Rudolf Höss, of Adolf
       Eichmann.
But I plead with you who do not speak:
       Stop being that dark and silent church. You must ask
       instead:
       "Am I complicit in my silence?"
Be that gravity that pulls billionaire space travelers back
to Earth.
Cry out for salmon, for orcas, for First Peoples!
Cry out, that I might crumble, that I shall fall so salmon may live.
Be that liberation; march your forces now.
Listen to the silent basaltic sentinel's promise on my behalf:
       I am not forever. Like colonialist man, I will not last
       much longer.
          And I cannot outlast the river.

PAUL E. NELSON

1047. Voluntary Hallucinations
4-August-22-Valerie Reynolds

**Tucson, AZ, Casa del Colibrí,
TUX woo' kwib, VALERIE!**

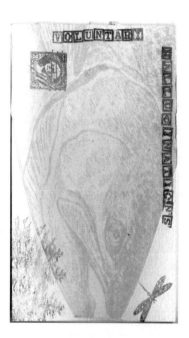

*Listening to running water is
a quick route to voluntary hallucination.*

Freeman House

"Totem Salmon" Freeman'd
call it. Bioregional canary for
watershed health. Orca food.
In the future we might
regard Columbia River dams
as voluntary hallucinations
as were the Elwha's & then
to remember to put the bones
of the first fish back.
Brothers! Study protocol!

PATRICK DIXON

Choices

We have to win every time. They only have to win once.

Jon Broderick, founder, The FisherPoets Gathering

We make our choices:
The Grand Coulee,
built for irrigation
of drought-burdened
farmland,
killed the salmon
running the Columbia.
June Hogs,
100-pound plus
Chinook salmon
swam for centuries
fed the first peoples
created culture and religion gone,
spawning grounds locked
forever behind concrete.

Dams killed sockeye, coho,
pink, and Chinook
throughout Washington.
Salmon fishing now
a ghost of what it was.
Phantom fish don't need
to spawn. Each dam
was a choice.

CHARLES PATTERSON

Tin Rock at Taylor Dock

Tourists pause to lean against rail,
focus cameras on its curves.
The ballerina statue, some call it, others
see yoga pose. The newspaper calls it *Grace,*
"a sculpture placed illegally at Taylor Dock."
Yet there she stands, right leg stretched,
defiant, curved behind arced back,
left arm horizoned over wine-dark
waves, gaze fixed on gray-blue islands.
Scrap metal wraps like ribbon
round legs, arms, belly, breasts.

Scrap metal tangles like ribbon
round workers' boots.
Boys shuffle, eyes down, backs slumped
over broom handles, mind's gaze
fixed on homes across the waves,
pushing tin through open door,
no pause permitted to watch it splash,
sink. Metallic sediments layer on ocean

floor, finally breaking surface.

A rock, it seems, as natural as salmon.

Graceful shrine to the nearly gone.

Bottom-Up

Plankton eaten by forage fish
forage fish dined on by Chinook salmon
Chinook salmon the southern-resident orca's exclusive diet
Southern-resident orca whales eat over 350 pounds of Chinook a day

Plankton
weakening
within Puget Sound

Sea level rise affects currents that
sweep away the sandy sediment
forage fish live in

glaciers melt
streams get less water
Puget Sound **Chinook salmon** *threatened*

MATTEO TAMBURINI

(We) Choose How It Ends

Again, they return to their stream
for the instinct to live rules supreme.
Our lives are entwined,
profit clouded our mind:
to redeem ourselves, break from its dream!

For countless generations
a generous celebration:
the orcas and bears
had plenty to share.
"Restore!" is my invocation.

To bring back the bounty of yore
as neighbors, we each have our chore:
the actions we'll take
this world to remake
together, we'll . . .

ROB LEWIS

Flotilla

October 3, 2015
For the Free the Snake Flotilla

There are three hundred people, young and old,
in canoes, rowboats, kayaks, and dinghies
streaming toward a dam.
The shimmering parchment hills
cradle their passage. A brass apple sun
showers its light.

And though the river is strangled, backed up,
sick with algae, it was once clean and bounding,
quivering with salmon, and that spirit
still lives and rises to meet the people
who come to release it.

How else to explain the bountiful grins and happy paddles,
chest howls and fist pumps, hull pounding
and paddle raising.

What sort of navy is this?

It's the earth's navy,
the admiralty of the heart.

Vigil

SASHA LAPOINTE

Salmon People Island

across mountains
in midsummer
I walked hand and hand
with my beloved
on a riverfront
in Eastern Washington

the day was hot and loud
the kind of crowded that always
made me into something
small and lonely
sterile art and kids
feeding ducks
families arguing
over ice cream

there were balloons
and politicians
ribbons and street food
my fingers wrapping
around his because
this kind of afternoon
makes me nervous
so he plucks a bloom
from a box and says
are you okay love
do want to stay
in the hotel room

but when I noticed words painted
on a wooden square
in the Salish language
it read Salmon People Island

and I was excited to find
something about this place
that I could recognize

so we chased the signs
along the pathways
and I was laughing
for the first time
that day

nevermind the dam
or the stranger who nearly
slammed into me
because I slowed my pace
when I saw the river
strangled beneath concrete

we had to navigate
and fight our way
through bodies
dodging strollers
and boys on skateboards
ducking and weaving
like we were swimming
like we were making
our way upstream

but when we finally
arrived to find the island
in that circle of trees
I felt something sink in me
all the way to the bottom
of some ocean floor
I hadn't even known
was inside of me

a grief long deepening
and cracking open

in my body
like a fresh cut
like blood blooming
across pavement

because Salmon People Island
was forgotten and empty
no manicured flower beds
no landscaping no children
with face paint or popsicles
or bands playing

I looked around the grounds
desolate and abandoned
this was the only part
in the whole of the park
left unattended

I watched a bag
float the branches
of a cedar tree
a little plastic ghost
caught dancing

I walked to the center
could hear the water
rushing over boulders
like it was trying
to break something

there are no more salmon
east of the mountains
and when I dropped
to my knees
he ran to my side
tried to retrieve
the dropped flower
he had given me

but he understood
when I told him
I couldn't stand
couldn't leave

I was afraid of losing
everything afraid
I'd never see another
Salmon Ceremony

and as the sun set
over the water
he brushed my hair
with his fingers
as he tried to convince me
I hadn't died

because I had forgotten
my name   my place   my body
and he picked me up
had to carry me
all the way back
to the parking lot
whispering quietly
in my ear
you're here   *you're here*   *you're here*

JOANNIE STANGELAND

This Is Not an Elegy

When I was a kid, I didn't like salmon,
admired the journey, not the taste.
A flavor I came to later.
What's loved too much, clutched,
becomes endangered.
One year, in memory, boats choked
the lake to hook the sockeye.
One year, a river so low, trucks
drove the salmon around a dam.
In the net of living, each tiny tear
unravels the rest. Say we can start
with mending, slow the warming,
say warming and mean drying up,
say we can save
the salmon, the orcas, the bears,
say salmon is more than a color,
say salmon, say water,
say river to stream,
say king, say finding,
say silver, say water,
say salmon, the damming,
the locks and ladders,
say water, say leaping,
say salmon, say running
in season, say finding,
say treaty, say salmon,
say water, say rights,
say finding, say streaming,
say salmon fighting,
drawn upstream,
say spawning and dying,
say salmon running
home.

EARLE THOMPSON

Vigil

I dip my net and the wooden pole
with its metal rim shivers.
The sky is still
as a salmon flutters upward
in the foaming water.
In midriver, salmon and water
merge on an ancient plane,
becoming momentarily
white.

The Columbia moves and swells
then spreads itself out
becoming a calm blue in my vision.

Celilo Falls' voice is a soft breeze
nestled in bleached bones
and haunting sagebrush
along the shore.

DIAN MILLION

The Highway

All the way down I-5 I hear the wheels underneath
the concrete we follow
they tell me the ice had barely retreated from the northern hemisphere
in the last millennium
when our people came to the river
in the spring we sang to the fish between the Tanana and the Columbia each leap of
wild water
a rain of silver so infinite
we believed
it could not end
we followed what the river told us murmuring in our sleep, answering the call,
answering each whisper from winged and finned
and antlered brethren into
all the seasons
all of our spirits mingled
on the banks
imprinted on the sides of
countless gorges and crevices
where the scaffolding
clings like spiderwebbing
old names
Minto
Celilo
we are parked along 84
on the Oregon side across from Cooks Landing
we can almost hear the dam we can hear the diesel trucks
from a long way off but i do not think you can hear
the salmon
my mother looks up the river
and i know she is listening
she hushes my little brother
who is playing with a toy diesel truck. we get back into the pickup
and return to the highway.

GEORGE SILVERSTAR

True Indian Modern Story

All an Indian needs to fish the Columbia is a motor boat, fifteen-hundred
feet of gillnet and a 30-30 to shoot back at the game wardens.

     Uncle Henry

My father is a little drunk and it delays our departure.
We will drive a hundred late summer miles to Celilo Falls.
My brother and I are keeping our heads down in the back seat.
My mother is pregnant and sensible and the discussion is
        unpleasant up front.
I have the impression this is a long-shot scheme.
We go anyway.

This is the last of Celilo's traditional fishing before the Dalles Dam
        project floods the grounds.
The falls are a natural drop in the Columbia River.
Forty-foot-high waterfalls and rock curve sharply into the body of
        the river where the wall of the basin nearly parallels
        the shore and slopes
downward until the river is flat again.

Pole platforms are built along the face.
Indians with long-handled dip nets are catching salmon which fail
        to make the summit and fall back.
The salmon struggle—almost swimming in air—shaking off scales
        and river water until quiet in the weave they are hauled
        into laps of many old gods.
Offer and goodbye, the Great Spirit has modern ideas.

There is smoke and flies and salmon drying on driftwood frames
        and innumerable Indian kids selling fish bigger
        than themselves.
We don't have the money to buy one.

Chief Tommy Thompson of the Yakima Nation makes his
        ceremonial appearance.
He is in a crowd of brown people who are all related.

He is in a beaded buckskin and full headdress.
He is old.
The Yakima Valley could be his daughter.

If my aunt were here we'd have a fish.
She has money because she doesn't have children.
That's what my mom says.
Her current man works on the railroad.
He's white.
They live in California.
She brought me a baseball mitt and a Japanese Swiss Army knife.
None of my relatives live in a teepee.

We go home and in the morning my dad the Indian goes to work
        in the mill.
We get a fish sometime after that.

CAITLIN SCARANO

Newhalem, Late October

*Newhalem is a company town owned by Seattle City Light and populated
entirely by employees of the Skagit River Hydroelectric Project*

Along the Trail of Cedars, the forest,
hemmed by fires in 1922
and 2015, dresses in stages of recovery,
regeneration.

Off the trail, I squeeze through
the seam of a hollowed out
western red cedar, *Thuja
plicata.* Heartwood
dead, the outer parts
still living. From that pitchy core,
I can see the fire-scarred
hillside, the first snow
dusting Davis Peak.

Not far from here, a huge boulder
overhangs a campsite used
by Upper Skagit Peoples
for more than 1,500 years.

Below the duff,
charred and split goat bones.

I count ten-foot-wide stumps
cut by hand with whipsaws.
Carved slots
for springboards where men
stood in the felling. Stands of old-

growth cedars and firs,
foliage rich with

nitrogen from decomposing
salmon. Trees fed on nutrients
from salmon can grow
three times higher.

Salmon like a bloodstream.
The sea is in the trees.

For decades representatives
from Seattle City Light said no salmon
came this far up river. Contradictions
braid like water. *To be frank*
they have cost the Upper Skagit enough;
100 years of degradation of our culture.
Near the base of Gorge Dam, I count
dozens of salmon carcasses, pale in
the stretch of last light. Aren't
we tired of speaking for?

TOM JAY

Elders

Salmon slap the work-scarred,
earth-curved decks of fish boats
like blind abandoned angels knocking
at a midnight door bereft . . .
The starry quicksilver glint of the sea
suffocating in our mortal air
and then
I've heard them slash the laughing rills
on moonless winter nights
dodging clawed phantoms
in the rock-creased stream.
But today watching
a water-bright bruise of dog salmon
brawl over this haunted gravel
for the first time in a decade . . .
I close my eyes and dream of
silver-skinned elders,
the old ones, spent and
weeping in welcome
for the clear-eyed rain.

LINDA MALNACK

The Salmon Contemplates Mortality

When death drops its hook, we think,
she disappeared and never came back;
he bled at the mouth and was gone—
we define them
by the cloud of blood, its shape. For a time,
they're ghosts in our midst; then we breathe in
what's left and go on, believing they
were out-translated
beyond the mirrored underside of reality
in which we see ourselves blurred. Oh, some
leap beyond the veil and come back still
living, strong ones
with stories of a place where we can breathe
only a moment, a bright silver moment
suspended in blue. They say sometimes
color isn't color
there—it's infused with light and a life
of its own—that the bottomless bottom
of that sea is black, punctured with small
bright holes.
They can't stay. Some law keeps them
here. Maybe it's only gravity, but maybe
gravity is a pseudonym for God. After all,
He is the Great
Author, and in his contract of obscurity—
to be fair—He writes in languages known
and unknown, even Salmon, written in red
within us.

DONALD MITCHELL

The Chinook

A fish so big even our hungry creek, swollen by rain,
can't swallow it. Fresh from the sea, its thick body
bronzed, dark freckling clear, no rotten patches or
ragged fins.

Only coho spawn here, so it's lost its way somehow.
It scares me a little, like a dead friend showing up
in a dream when you don't know it's a dream,
and you know it's both wrong and inevitable. Dangerous,
it feels, a live torpedo washed up in the surf from a war
fought long ago and far away.

I want to share this feeling, this fear, so I run to fetch
my brother and friend, but when I return with them,
it's gone. All that's left: a deep sound: boulders thumping
under the ribs of the flood.

ALICIA HOKANSON

Salmon Leap

Mirror of cloud, last light
off the mountains taking
the colorless water.

How did he come to that flight?
Was it desire,
a glinting fly
that pulled him?

Heaven above,
below: the spinning planet
lost in myth.

To those depths
does he take
a vision to haunt him?
A world dissolving
in so much light
and he
a gasping stranger there?

TEGAN KEYES

The Cycle

The salmon died
in a shallow wing
of the river

and already
the body's scales
are flaking away
in rainbows,

and bacterial specks
are clustering upon it
like fine dust on a silver needle
worn from its work.

It has pierced many miles of water,
stitching together the river
and the salt-stiff fabric of the sea.

A single thread
in a tapestry weaving through

the orca's teeth, the heron's beak,
the eagle's plunging talons,
the bear's dark gut,
the tangled roots of cedar and spruce,

and now the glittering moss of microbes
frilling across the tired body
tarnished green and red

which has accomplished
nothing less
than the mending
of the world.

LUTHER ALLEN

it is wrong to wreck the world

i was born unto salmonidae
line in the water   waiting the sudden
orgasm of strike from the wet of mystery
explosion into the deadly air as curl of flapping light
condensed   elemental   bursting
into this other world as ecstatic energy
as totem   as icon   as sustenance

this was felt   without thought
                    now i live among the salmon people

            i could answer to that same name

i pray by fishing   casting into infinity for an answer
so do the salmon people   i imagine   i hope
the salmon answers by swimming

                        into the net
                        into the jaws
                                of the orca

                into the net

                others escape
                to the headwaters of everything
                to die and return

the prayer   the answer
again and again

their flesh unto   *ursus americanus   ursus arctos horribilis*
                        haliaeetus leucocephalus   corvus corax   larus glaucescens
                        maggots   molecules   minerals   cedar   fir   salal
                        salmon people   me

their eggs   pilfered by whitefish   trout
                    some born unto the wet
                    the light of mystery
                    the death heat we are making
                    the suffocation   the darkness

prayers gone dry

VICTOR ORTIZ

we are you

thunderclap!

        through a crack in a creek

out salmon   leap

      onward

       homeward

   living beings can smell their beginnings

          long before the nonexistent existed
            before sky split from earth
            before air streamed like rivers
            before rivers became homes

              in that time
              the salmon people
              first made humans
              from bones and their skins

                taught us what to sing
                how to ensure their eternal return
                to feed on their effervescent flesh

  we are you
          salmon sing as they swim upstream

  we are you
          our song of welcome and thanks

EUGENE MARCKX

Deep Sea Salmon

Dad where have you gone?
Did you leap quicksilver into the last run
of legendary kings—those eighty-pound June Hogs—
that bashed themselves against the walls
of the Grand Coulee Dam?
Or are you too smart for the trap of extinction
still holding in the shadows of that dam
in the back of my mind—thinking
but not showing much?

Once in a while I hear your voice
and I'll catch a quiet grin in your tone
After all our wrong guesses about each other
I ask again—Is it me you like or is it
just the old charm you turn on
to glove a hard bargain?

When your dad came around
did you cover up or trade him blows?
Or maybe you leapt his trap too
and thought yourself free
No you didn't beat me but his fist
was still in your hand held back
You couldn't quite bless anything I did
All the bright eyes you praised
but never your son
Or was it a stone you couldn't explain
that praise breaks hollow against hard luck—
luck that always runs out?

But sometimes out of our long fishing past
you come in behind me whispering
Let your line go where the current runs against itself

and what may not be there can come into play
Then again if the tide takes you over the bar
I'll be looking for you off the coast
flashing up from the deep

MATTHEW ROBERTS

The Inlet

In the mist, you dissolve questions.
There's no circling back.
You keep casting, stripping line,
squinting into gray space
knowing lights and smoke
are somewhere lost
in port towns of your imagination.

The only constant is doubt
reminding you there is luck and no luck
fly fishing for coho in the salt.
You keep at it because
what the hell else should you be doing?
You can't quit now.
"The tug is the drug," they say.

Fishing isn't always about fishing.
It's shedding layers
of what you carry.
When you wade the point
reading water for signs
of sand lance or herring—
nothing and everything goes by.

And you see these worlds converge,
and your place within them.
Something will turn
as you consider possibilities,
disappointments,
and how the night drifts on
whether you're there or not.

TESS GALLAGHER

Ambition

for my brother Tom

We had our heads down
baiting hooks—three wild salmon
already turned back that morning
for the in-season hatchery silvers
now out there somewhere
counting their luck—when
under our small boat the sea
gave a roll like a giant turning over

in sleep, lifting us high so I thought
an ocean liner or freighter had
slipped up on us, the sudden heft
of its bow-wave, our matchstick toss
to depth we'd taken
for granted in order to venture there
at all. But when I looked up expecting
collision, the quash of water from their

blowholes pushed to air in unison,
a pair of gray whales not two hundred
yards away: "Look up!" I shouted so you
didn't miss the fear-banishing
of their passage that made
nothing of us. Not even death could touch
any mind of us. It was all beauty and
mystery, the kind that picks you up

effortlessly and darts through you
for just those moments
you aren't even there. Held that way
and their tons-weight bodies plunged

silently under again, I turned for proof
to you, but the clarity was passing through
as a swell under us again and the sky of the sea
set us down like a toy.

And that's the way it was, and it wasn't
any other way—just looking at each other,
helpless one thought and huge with power
the next. We baited up,
dropped our herring into slack water—
two ghosts fishing for anything but whales.

AMY GULICK

Fade

Tell me what it means
To belong to a home stream
I no longer know

The salmon are gone
The soul of the river drowned
I have lost my way

Tell me what it means
To give thanks to a home stream
I no longer know

Adrift from the fish
A castaway of the land
What do I do now?

ALICE DERRY

Finding the Poem

After twenty-five years on the Olympic Peninsula,
we watch coho jump the Soleduck cascades

Solil'tak: Quilleute for sparkling water

"I'm good," you say, and go back to the car.
How differently we need things—

I could be here until dark comes down, or rain,
each fish making me content
to wait as long as I need to,
until the next catapults skyward.

It's not what we're allowed to call *will,*
but they're up for it,
slapping against the rocks
if their aim isn't in line with the surging down-current,
or landing in a shallow dish on top,
which leads nowhere.
A futile surge forward, then
they let themselves be washed back and down.

Some slip up the sides of this narrow chute,
or sluice through. Some shoot dead center—
ruby bodies nothing but muscle,
heads iridescent green.

So much takes place below what's churned white,
I can't tell which fish make it
and which must accept over and over
a fall to slack water.

The boiling on a rock shelf,
full of thrashing tails, has to be the next step.
Maybe ten miles, all they have left
of the sixty they can reach up this river
to channels and springs of their birth and spawning.

Strands of silver stitching together our world,
my friend writes. We know their story,
carrying heart's blood high into the mountains,
feeding animals and trees
before sending their fry spiraling down
to saltwater again.

Somewhere I read how difficult it is,
their change to ocean. Like being smothered.

"Discouraging," you say, when I come to the car—
"everything's going in one direction
and you're going in another."

"They don't feel that way," I say.
"Salmon are built for their stream."
"OK." You let go quietly. I don't press my point
as I usually do. "Stay as long as you want," you say.

We've lost three parents in a short time—
our arms raised, warding off blows.
We're tender with one another.

So I go back.

I go back to watch how, water-bound
and trying every other course first,
they launch and fly,
paddling air,
bringing to its indifferent pressure—its lassitude,
which can't receive hard rowing,

but asks for the lightness of bird-bone—
what they have to offer water:

mushing through
as far as they can go. Farther.

What We Owe

GLORIA BIRD

What We Owe

Rain fanning its gray light early over an eastern sky could be the tail of
some great salmon in the river of history. The sun comes up bright
forgetfulness. Sometimes the mind perverts the natural cycles clamping shut
around its petty denials and all things we refuse to bring into the present
with us. Freud knew the consequence of muffled history, yet continued to lie
about it, to disguise the one truth that might have liberated us all. I know
what I owe to women whose fingers were rubbed raw digging roots on some
northwestern plain. Maybe they were on-the-run or preparing the ceremonial
wake for the camas fields that would be replaced in their lifetimes by miles
of wheat. The land there bears our pain, and there is no cleansing only stark
refusals like the river receding from jutting rock. Back then, I did not
understand how the old people endured that sad place along the Tshimakain
where they would eat and tell stories beneath the pine trees. In a tender
fleshy place called inheritance, like an old wound healed over a small stone,
begins this long understanding, the way the bones of sleek animals that fed
generations belong to the river, are returned to those liquid beginnings to
communicate our need to those living there. To the earth goes the innermost
heart of the heart in which the essence of deer mingle with that of our
ancestors in this continuum where what we owe, we owe, and pass on to our
children.

PRISCILLA LONG

Memo to the Columbia River

You are a domesticated dragon,
your violent rapids flooded, calmed,
your fishing cliffs drowned,

your salmon ground up in turbines.
You are a long tongue reaching
for the sea, where you return

to turmoil and treachery, your roiling
currents rocking the bones of drowned
sailors. When we who tamed you are

gone—some say extinction for us
within one hundred years—may you destroy
your dams. May your waters flash

and sing once again, your salmon
teem and spawn high in your highest
reaches. May Roosevelt Lake

with the irrevocable power of water
breach Grand Coulee Dam, return
the sacred fishing grounds to the gods.

CARLA SHAFER

Every River

How long the memory of stream scent
or flavor of home is carried beneath scales,
in the wave of a silvery fin.

Even after bulldozers raze a riverbank,
and currents forced to flow underground,
salmon seek home, yet they must mark

time while the river cools. The estuary
becomes a stasis where hunger grows
and fishers set their nets.

Kept from gravel beds for laying and
fertilizing eggs, salmon's life cycle breaks.
Fish runs decline. Orcas starve.

We can change, become protectors,
or we too are condemned to wait in the shallows
where breath is weak and voices silent, and

we feel the shroud conceal a redeemable future,
wither as the mindscape of spirit fades, lose
the path home beneath gray rain.

SHIN YU PAI

trout creek ≅ little water

in Roxhill Park, I pull the ribbon
of connection, scout your headwaters

buried long ago beneath storm
drain and sewage pipe,

follow posted trail markers
across asphalt lots emitting heat

past unshaded ball fields to spring outward in a thicket of shade,

unburied behind the community gardens,
the turn of water moving over stone—

salmon counted returning to swim
again along the legacy trail,

the tributary at first daylight

SCOTT FERRY

when i first moved to seattle

i could feel the salmon coursing under the streets
i could feel their voices as the seasons swept in—
       first rough wind of september on the puget sound
       golden gardens gray with gull sand flat and unpeopled
       first snow wetclumped in the false lights crow calling without echo
       first salmonberry flowers as bright as a hummingbird throat
i knew there was a text under the rain on glass a speechless speaking
i could feel the surging of something spawning under the cement
       where the rivers had been throated in pipes
       where the languages had been rerouted onto graveyards
       where the screens scream nothing into a paved boil
i could feel each fish slip under me with a pop—
       the ancestors of ocean to river to ocean to river
       now in a sea under this sea
and the voices still slap against my ribs from the inside
       their children still breaking currents in the cedar river
       still smelling markers in rivermouths of last year's deaths and births
       still feeding the thin orca still redfleshed and silver—
the silver of the stars in december the silver
       of cities underground

Daylighting Thornton Creek

Little thought given to building over, paving over
the two branches of northeast Seattle's Thornton Creek
and a myriad of streamlets. Early settlers with expansive hopes
of bland prosperity absconded with the land from tribes.
In the early 1890s, one-third of Washingtonians worked
in the lumber industry. Farms. Houses. Meadowbrook Golf Course
on which land now sits a high school. Then came the interstate.

The sequalae has us bemoaning buildup of sediment
and how salmon spawning became a used-to-be. My taxes
build retention ponds to mitigate flooding in the city.
Basements and the high school leak. It's a given
and a sump pump heaven. Now we try to daylight streams
even close to houses to bring the salmon population back
to what the city fathers let us squander.

It was common knowledge that everything leaked.

> I am walking along Wallingford
> aware there is a stream
> in a culvert   close   coursing
> under front yards from Licton Springs.
> My city cracks concrete,
> digs dirt to surface streams,
> builds footpath bridges for those who stroll.

It's difficult to undo damage but sometimes we try

> so that frog, newt, duck,
> migratory bird, beaver, and coyote
> again traipse riparian traces.
> Finally, in 2018, Chinook salmon
> were seen returned to spawn,

to redd, nest deep in gravel before dying
so their offspring could live to do the same.

One might say our city is getting with the program for land and water stolen from the Duwamish, Suquamish, Stillaguamish, and Muckleshoot. Cannot erase what has been done. In truth, would I return my own house with leaky basement on land that was not the banker's right to sell me? Complicated stories in countries and in families. Sunlight stipples wet grasses shimmering in the rocky riffle. Much like salmon, collectively we spawn, guard our tiny pockets of roe, tucked in gravel where water runs clear.

Chum Return to Johns Creek at Bayshore Preserve

When the chum returns to Johns Creek in November, we celebrate!

Ask the Squaxin Island Tribe, Steh-Chass (Lushootseed), whose ancestral waters and tidelands dwell in all seven of the southernmost inlets of the Salish Sea. People of the Water, not of any river. Tribal fishers herd chum into nets as they swim over mud flats, past salt marshes and estuaries into the mouths of creeks to spawn. Salmon are sacred and honored in ceremony with their first arrival. Johns Creek, on Hammersley Inlet, Sa-Heh-Wa-Mish (Lushootseed) is ready.

The Steh-Chass tell us chum are the most muscular salmon, thus
they are honored to catch them in their nets. Chum have returned
to the Sa-Heh-Wa-Mish since time immemorial. There is more to say:

> After the Medicine Creek Treaty of 1854 was signed,
> *The People say it was the time the world turned upside down.*

Bayshore Peninsula had the biggest longhouse in the southern Salish Sea—
that longhouse was burned down. Settlers flocked to Mason County.
Where there were forests, there were logging camps.
Where there were running creeks, soon a mill with a flume was built.
Where there was land, there were towns built with that lumber.

Johns Creek kept flowing. Chum kept returning. Despite
a mill on its mouth that would later be dismantled to create
the Bayshore Golf Club, the chum return. When the salt marsh
was diked to create larger fairways with a water view, chum worked
harder to return home. When the landowners siphoned the creek
to irrigate the fairways, the salmon thrashed up to spawn.

In 2014 the Capitol Land Trust bought these seventy-four acres and named it Bayshore Preserve. A place to visit a pristine salt marsh, and a restored spawning creek with quiet channels dug in its estuary to allow smolts to survive before returning to the ocean. A land trust is designed to allow the land to return to its right side up self. This November, the chum return to Johns Creek and we welcome them home.

MARTHA SILANO

In a Font Called Avenir Book,

I try to explain Nacho's sandpaper tongue,
how she stretches her paw along my arm.

She is gray, pale orange, warm, and already
I'm failing. Outside, the scratchy calls of jays

undulating past the fir that blocks our view
of an active volcano (it's not dormant;

its vents release steam, the inevitable landslidejacks
that will bury Enumclaw and Sumner, its ash

once again reaching Puget Sound). The font says
shek shek shek, but its rake-ier, squawkish.

Also, *keesh keesh keesh,* eliciting nostalgia
as if I'm ninety-nine, surveying my life, realizing

the best parts were quiet enough to hear the birds,
overcast afternoons when the trees stood still

and the words of far-off voices could be discerned.
Quiet enough to consider Commencement Bay,

where the Puyallup people fattened up on a glut
of salmon they could walk across, where

Simpson Tacoma Kraft erected a paper mill
requiring 40,000 dump-truck loads to cart away

its deadlier-than-Lake-Erie-when-it-caught-on-fire
sludge. To consider the Duwamish River.

My husband floats it during the biyearly humpy run;
we eat those fish because, he tells me, they never

touch bottom. PCBs, arsenic, dioxins, sewage,
and petroleum under a rayless orange sun,

a single common tansy, humble bloom that doesn't
blind, shrouded in smoke. The haze we know

like our own bodies, its vents, its faults, its uncontainable
fires quadrupling in a matter of hours, an entire region

given a red flag warning. That kind of dry fuel,
that kind of potential for being licked.

EDWARD HARKNESS

Midnight Midpoint of the Cedar River Bridge

Over the guardrail, some twenty feet down, Chinook salmon—
hundreds, thousands—floated, their spent bodies bluish

under the garish light of sodium lamps. More cars, more semis
than I'd have guessed at that hour. Passing under the bridge,

belly up, drifting sideways, the Chinooks tumbled, luminous,
current-caught, bumping into themselves, already in decay

after their labors to get here, charging past dams, clear-cuts,
factory spills, their silver sides gouged, fins ripped off, tails torn—

all to find Cedar River gravel beds and be, once more, reborn.
Downstream, they will feed bears, minks, eagles, gulls, flies.

Behind my back, traffic roared. The rail hummed in my hands.
Who are they, these drivers? Coming or going? From where

to where? The sidewalk itself trembled. Below: a silent procession.
Up here: a cacophony of cars, headlights, stink of diesel exhaust.

Mad thought: I wanted to block traffic, implore irate drivers
to roll down their windows to hear my lecture on the beauty

of salmon, the perfection of their migration, the precision
of their memory. *Just for two minutes,* I'd say in my calmest voice,

turn off your engines. I swear I'm harmless. Go to the rail.
Look down. Those are the salmon people. Please thank them.

They have been feeding the world for thousands of years. That's it.
Bid them well and return to your cars. The dead are swimming home.

PAUL LINDHOLDT

Ode on a Granite Slab

Where fish once flashed upstream, the river sprays.
Spring spawners strained where abject people
now give intention to Galileo's law of parabolic fall.
Angry verses spiral in granite beside the street.

If nets stretched from the Monroe Street Bridge
deck, they would catch human jumpers, just as
nets captured salmon before the advent of the dams.
Laden places vibrate with every shred of violence

and love ever bred there, or so fringe theories hold.
Places echo and shudder with longing and loss
beneath the soil. The dead can dance
and teach survivors how to swirl, how to clomp

to the tunes sent leaking from those fraught spots.
Monuments to conquerors agitate the soil.
Tear them down. Rename parks and streets
to placate Clio. Lay those shaken spirits to rest.

The poet bridled an abiding anger about a shattered past.
From the poem the word *love* erupts eight times.
How can the First People ever come to love again
when the jumping salmon all are ghosts?

FIG DEPAOLO

150 Chinook Salmon Released into the Spokane River on August 24, 2022

There is evidence to suggest that
life is still attainable, even in slow doses.
Even when drip fed. Even when the walk is swept
of evidence, even when one thousand cars spit gravel by
I have seen vibrance, and I have seen
mouths spread in song, I have
been listening to every sincere effort, and I know
it is ridiculous to assume we cannot right our path.
Watch this. I will take a step, to show that so can you.
So you can look me in the eyes and mean it.
So you can say, You know where you are?
and mean it. You know. Land back. Mean it.
Now let me show you these
northern reaches of the Columbia River Basin
and the river that flows from my eyes
and into my mouth—no
salmon have lived here since 1911
when the Little Falls Dam went up.
But here they are again. I wanted
to write about my home. Undeniably.
In such a concrete way. Know where you are?
Where it is beautiful here, again, and because of?
Chinook salmon, in the sharp water, I remember
all those years you were not here.
Just as I remember all those years you were,
busy, like choking on laughter, in the water
which clings to you, which listens
to your breathing. It is significant
to have gone and returned.
But you know that.

THENA WESTFALL

How I Became an Environmentalist

shivering in the bow of your boat, my small frame
obscured by life-jacket orange, I found mercy
every Sunday from early spring to late fall

we never spoke of God, only of fish
you taught me that helping requires a firm grip
our lives wound tight against the reel

the line making tidy trips down and back
later I'd learn life is more like backlash
you pull and pull but never get it right

your Zen, dedication to predawn brisk
out here it is clean, the art of quiet
must be learned before one can observe

nature is not a picture protected by glass
as you worked the slick line fast,
knots for hooks and swivel, I began

to understand
even fish deserve respect
now I think of salmon

struggling upstream in search of death, each year less
make this journey, it changes
to memory, yet somehow everyone has tasted

salmon, but until you have raised club to wriggling temple
and committed
will you really know how it tastes

TELE AADSEN

I Whisper Anyway

The new-penny scent of king salmon is heavy in the air as I slide steel beneath gill plate, slicing feathery tissue so unlike my own lungs. We die the same, in crimson bursts from busted pipes. Blood pools around her body as I trace a finger down the amethyst lateral line. My glove leaves a trail of flat aluminum, her color already fading like a dream.

"Thank you." I whisper this knowing it doesn't matter. Speaking sweet to salmon in the water, thanking them in the boat: these are rituals ridiculous to many of my colleagues, and to me, too, sometimes. This fish is dead by my hand, with many more to follow. I whisper anyway. Even as we make our living taking these lives, I want to always remember a salmon's value is not its price per pound. Salmon are more than a commodity; they are silver-robed ambassadors of home and hope, risk and return. They are ancestors shared across cultures, linking sea and land; the matchmaking elders who bring so many of us together. They are gods creating and sustaining us, one fish at a time.

The Use of Weapons

My grandmother said that in Kentucky men
Went gigging—spearing—fish or, maybe, sometimes,
Dynamiting. Only gigging was legal.
Here I watch video of a young Native
Man who, in canoes he builds, hooks salmon on
Two-pronged spears. Where I was born, in Japan, a

Fishing boat called *Lucky Dragon* came home, in
1954, covered in white ash from
A thermonuclear bomb tested in the
Pacific, eighty-six miles away but more
Powerful than predicted. A man died. His
Tuna would have died anyway, being caught

And eaten, being irradiated—would
They care? Would the fish in Kentucky prefer
Gigging or exploding? Yet I believe the
Salmon here care, because the young man who carves
His boats says he honors them. I believe they
Try to taste good for him, to honor him back.

Transplanted Prayers

Amo Adawehi
Water Bringers
Listen to me!

UlaGa Amoyinehi
Chief of the Spirits
Who dwell in the water
Grandfather recognize me!

Ancient Rainmakers
Hear me!
Use your sacred formulas now.

Bring out your war clubs
and tortoise-shell rattles to battle
The forces of drought and despair.

We came from the place of the Red People
Down where Tsalagi roots run deep

To here, this place of the Salmon People
Where the old ones have hitched a ride.

Dry creeks. Hot rivers. Algae lakes.

Mother Ocean suffering, suffering

We are all suffering.

Heed the Song of Salmon
Restlessly waiting, testing, tasting
Gambling on one last desperate push.

We can do no less if we want to survive.

SCOTT T. STARBUCK

Three Sockeye in Columbia River, Oregon

The first had no eyes.
The second no tongue.
The third fungus gills.

"Salmon people have spoken,"
said the fisherman
to others who stared in disbelief.

Finally, someone asked,
"What did they say?"
"Water is too hot to survive,

and you're next.
Unless you listen and change,
the curse you put on us

will be on you, and your children."

What Salmon Need: A Meditation on Place

A shallow pool stretches among gray stones along the river margin. The pool trembles with the faintest of raindrops—drops as faint as breath, drops so fine they barely pluck the surface tension of the water. I gaze past leafy reflections, searching the pool for movement. At first there is only the gentle stirring of caddisfly larvae on the bottom of the pool, then the sudden skate of a water strider. Finally, I see the wary movement of a small fish as it swims closer to the stillness of my shadow. I shift my position and the fish rushes to safety in a crevice between the rocks. When it emerges again, I admire the delicate ruffling movements of its fins and tail, the elusive quality of its coloring, its tiny size. Perhaps only something this minute can sense the thrumming of faint rain.

Just weeks ago this young salmon was nestled in riverbed gravel somewhere upstream, nearing the end of its miraculous transformation from egg to fish. It emerged from the gravel and was washed downstream to this protected channel margin. Here in the small pool, the little fish lives entirely in this moment, reacting to every shadow, waiting for drifting food. It is oblivious to the Endangered Species Act. It has no inkling that tribal identities and human livelihoods hang in the balance of its survival. It is unaware that this pool may dry up. It is not consciously preparing for its future journey to the ocean, or for its return to spawn in this river. Yet the fulfillment of the next generation of salmon is represented by the survival of this tiny, fragile, unhurried fish.

I am not personally capable of seeing that this fish survives. I can't cradle it, or feed it, or nurse it to health if it fails to thrive. I cannot be here to guard it from predators or to shoo it to the river if the water recedes. Instead, I am asked to embrace the context of its existence, where Pacific wrens fill the air with song and water seeps down mossy banks; where the otter hunts and thrushes whistle from cedar boughs; where alders form a leafy canopy and the surge of high water creates side channels; where trees fall to form pools and backwaters; where intermittent streams spill last year's decomposing leaves.

Many of us will attend meetings and hearings to decide the fate of salmon. Some of us will hammer out agreements and laws. A few are wise enough to advise others on the nuances of salmon biology. But surely one need is for more of us to stand in the presence of a stream and comprehend the intricate wildness that salmon must have to begin and end their lives.

JANE ALYNN

The Green Place

This is where I go when the rain stops.
I walk next to the stream,
a boggy, narrow corridor
of seamless rocks, verdant with moss,
through ancient evergreens and arches
of broadleaf trees that enshrine me.
I grieve for the dwindling wetlands, the salmon
who need, like me, cool, hidden places,
quiet-water edges to recover themselves.
Humankind has not helped them—
rapacious, without mercy, and only half in.
I want to believe that someday,
caring as never before, we'll see the
whole of it.

EM ARATA-BERKEL

Branching

like veins,   rivers flow
red with
       ripened bodies
         bucking, striving
against snowmelt   to   create their own
    p u s h b a c k   ~~damned~~
        up waterfalls
         t o w a r d
         the wellspring,
         where beginnings
         become ends
        become
      beginnings
   flowing
like   all   things
to   a   boundless   silver   sea

RICHARD REVOYR

Future of Hope

A moth, anchored to the web of a spider, speaks:

"There is no hope."

A spawned-out salmon, drifting across her redd, speaks:

"There is only hope."

There is no hope

                    There is only hope

There is no hope

                    There is only hope

There is no hope

                    There is only hope

                    There is only hope

                    There is only hope

                    There is only hope

Acknowledgments

The editor and publisher gratefully acknowledge the permissions granted to reproduce the copyrighted material in this collection. Every effort has been made to trace copyright holders and obtain their permission. The publisher apologizes for any errors or omissions in the following list and would like to be notified of any corrections for future reprints.

Gabrielle Bates, "Salmon" originally appeared in The American Poetry Review (May/June 2021) and will appear in the book Judas Goat, Tin House, 2023. Used with the permission of the author.

Scott Bentley, "The sʔuladxw Map of Seattle" was displayed alongside work from Rena Priest as part of the exhibition Submergence: Going Below the Surface with *Orca and Salmon* at the Jack Straw Cultural Center, Seattle, June 1–30, 2021.

Jim Bertolino, "Salmon Breathing" was published in *Ravenous Bliss: New & Selected Love Poems,* MoonPath Press. Copyright © 2014, 2020 Jim Bertolino. Used with the permission of the author.

Gloria Bird, "What We Owe" is from *The River of History,* Trask House Books. Copyright © 1998 by Gloria Bird. Reprinted with permission of the author.

Pamela Hobart Carter, "In the Paintings of Alfredo Arreguín . . ." appears on the Museum of Northwest Art's website, www.monamuseum.org/.

Raymond Carver, "At Night the Salmon Move" is from *Fires,* 1983. Copyright © 1976 Raymond Carver, 1996 Tess Gallagher, used by her permission.

Alice Derry, "Finding the Poem" was first published in *Windfall: A Journal of Poetry of Place* and also appears in *Tremolo,* Red Hen Press, 2012, redhen.org. Used with the permission of the author.

Patrick Dixon, "Choices" was published in *National Fisherman,* May 2018.

Tess Gallagher, "Ambition" is from *Is, Is Not.* Copyright © 2019 by Tess Gallagher. Reprinted with the permission of The Permissions Company, LLC on behalf of the author and Graywolf Press, Minneapolis, Minnesota, graywolfpress.org.

Sierra Golden, "Triangulation" first appeared in *The Seattle Review of Books,* March 8, 2016, and is included in *The Slow Art,* Bear Star Press, 2018. Used with the permission of the author.

Meagan Graves, "Anadromous" was first published in Gonzaga University's *Reflection,* vol. 63 (Spring 2022).

Alicia Hokanson, "Salmon Leap" is from *Mapping the Distance,* Breitenbush Books, Portland, OR, 1989. Used with the permission of the author.

Tom Jay, "Elders" is from *The Blossoms Are Ghosts at the Wedding,* Empty Bowl Press, 2019. Used by permission of Empty Bowl Press.

Georgia Johnson, "Before I Knew Salmon" was published by Desert Rose Press and Clifford Burke. Used with the permission of the author.

Shelley Kirk-Rudeen, "What Salmon Need: A Meditation on Place" appeared in the May 1998 issue of *South Sound Green Pages,* a publication of the South Puget Environmental Education Clearinghouse (SPEECH), Olympia, WA.

Rob Lewis, "Flotilla" and "I Went Looking for the Wild One" are from *The Silence of Vanishing Things.* Copyright © 2017 Rob Lewis. Reprinted with the permission of the author.

Linda Malnack, "The Salmon Contemplates Mortality" was published in *Christianity & Literature* 48, no. 3 (Spring 1999); reprinted in *Christianity & Literature* 50, no. 3 (Spring 2001) and in *Imago Dei: Poems from Christianity & Literature,* Abilene Christian University Press, 2012.

C.R. Manley, "Pinned": a version of this poem appeared in *Windfall: A Journal of Poetry of Place* 20, no. 2 (Spring 2022).

Christen Mattix, "Record Salmon Run" appeared in *For the Love of Orcas: An Anthology,* ed. Andrew Shattuck McBride and Jill McCabe Johnson, Wandering Aengus Press, 2019, and in *Psaltery & Lyre,* October 2014, www.dovesand serpents.org/wp/2014/10/104-psaltery-lyre-christen-mattix-record-salmon-run-at-mattole-river/.

Phelps McIlvaine, "Water by Salmon" was published on *The Poetry Department . . . aka The Boynton Blog,* www.thepoetrydepartment.wordpress.com/2019/08/18/water-by-salmon/.

Mary McMinn, "Passionate Water Poem" appears in *Watershed Poems,* Homestead Press, Ellensburg, WA, 1997. Used with the permission of the author.

Dian Million, "The Highway" appears in *Dancing on the Rim of the World: An Anthology of Contemporary Northwest Native American Writing,* ed. Andrea Lerner. Tucson: Sun Tracks and University of Arizona Press, 1990. Originally published in *Mr. Cogito: The American Indian Special Issue* VIII, no. 3 (1988), ed. John M. Gogol and Robert A. Davies. Used with the permission of the author.

Donald Mitchell, "The Chinook" is included in the book *Strays,* 2022.

Nancy Pagh, "Spring Salmon at Night" was published in *No Sweeter Fat,* Autumn House Press, Pittsburg, PA, 2007. Reprinted with permission of the author.

Shin Yu Pai, "trout creek ≅ little water" appeared in *ENSŌ,* Entre Rios, 2020. Used with the permission of the author.

Jennifer Preston, "Lateral Lines" first appeared in the Echology Poetry Walk Project, Gig Harbor, WA, 2021.

Susan Rich, "Food for Fallen Angels" was first published in *Gallery of Postcards and Maps: New and Selected Poems,* Salmon Poetry, 2022. Used with the permission of the author.

Judith Roche, "Salmon Suite" was published in *Wisdom of the Body,* Black Heron Press, 2007. Used by permission of Black Heron Press.

George Silverstar, "True Indian Modern Story" first appeared in *Dalmo'ma #2,* 1978. It was included in Silverstar's posthumous collection *Silverstar,* Sagittarius Press, Port Townsend, WA, 1992. The poem later appeared in *Working the Woods Working the Sea,* Empty Bowl Press, 2008.

Ann Spiers, "Dressing" appears in *Salmon Flash Silver in Her Net,* Laughing Dog Press, Vashon Island, WA, 1984. Used with the permission of the author.

Scott T. Starbuck, "Three Sockeye in Columbia River, Oregon" first appeared in *Windfall: A Journal of Poetry of Place* (Spring 2022), www.hevanet.com/windfall/, and also on riverseek.blogspot.com, March 16, 2022, www.riverseek.blogspot.com /2022/03/three-sockeye-in-columbia-river-oregon.html.

Sarah Stockton, "Salt and Other Spells" was first published in *Luna Luna Magazine* in 2019, www.lunalunamagazine.com/blog/poetry-by-sarah-stockton?rq=Sarah%20Stockton/. This poem is also included in the chapbook *Time's Apprentice,* dancing girl press, 2021.

Robert Sund, "Salmon Moon" is from *Poems from Ish River Country: Collected Poems and Translations,* Counterpoint Press, 2004.

Earle Thompson, "Vigil" appears in *Dancing on the Rim of the World: An Anthology of Contemporary Northwest Native American Writing,* ed. Andrea Lerner. Tucson: Sun Tracks and University of Arizona Press, 1990. Reprinted with permission.

Richard Tice, "jumbled fish nets" is included in *Four Hundred and Two Snails: HSA Members' Anthology,* ed. by Nicholas Sola. Haiku Society of America, 2018, p. 105.

Gail Tremblay, "Comparing Sockeye and King Salmon" is from *Indian Singing: Poems,* CALYX Press. Copyright © 1990, 1998. Reprinted with the permission of the author.

Thena Westfall, "How I Became an Environmentalist" was published in a different version in *Tidepools,* 2009. Used with the permission of the author.

Maya Jewell Zeller, "Socioeconomic" was originally published in *Ecotone* and appeared in the collection *Rust Fish,* Lost Horse Press, 2011. Used with the permission of the author.

Notes

Scott Bentley, "The sʔuladxʷ Map of Seattle": sʔuladxʷ is the dxʷləšucid (Snohomish Lushootseed) word translating to salmon.

Gabriela Denise Frank, "(yubəč / chinook)": Sources for passages in this poem: "Downstream": "Pregnancy was an erasure of the self. A person was turned by impregnation into both miracle and meat," Anne Enright, "A Cruel Vote," *New York Review of Books,* May 8, 2022; "Mothering is a net of living threads to lovingly encircle what it cannot possibly hold, what will eventually move through it," Robin Wall Kimmerer, *Braiding Sweetgrass: Indigenous Wisdom, Scientific Knowledge, and the Teachings of Plants;* "We think back through our mothers if we are women," Virginia Woolf, *A Room of One's Own.* "Upstream": "I want vast distances. My savage intuition of myself," Clarice Lispector, *Stream of Life;* "No feeling is final," Rainer Maria Rilke, "Go to the Limits of Your Longing," trans. Joanna Macy; "We look at the world once in childhood, the rest is memory," Louise Glück, "Nostos"; "The journey itself is my home," Bashō.

Ann Batchelor Hursey, "Chum Returns to Johns Creek at Bayshore Preserve": Bayshore Preserve is located on the Bayshore Peninsula, off Oakland Bay, Mason County, Washington, and is part of the Capitol Land Trust, Olympia.

Deirdre Lockwood, "Three Salmon Redactions": "Mortal": From Tian, Zhenyu et al. "A Ubiquitous Tire Rubber–Derived Chemical Induces Acute Mortality in Coho Salmon." *Science* vol. 371,6525 (2021): 185–189. doi:10.1126/science.abd6951. Reprinted with permission from AAAS. "Home scent": From Williams, Chase R et al. "Elevated CO_2 Impairs Olfactory-Mediated Neural and Behavioral Responses and Gene Expression in Ocean-Phase Coho Salmon (Oncorhynchus kisutch)." *Global Change Biology* vol. 25,3 (2019): 963–977. doi:10.1111/gcb.14532. "Elwha": From Duda, Jeffrey J et al. "Reconnecting the Elwha River: Spatial Patterns of Fish Response to Dam Removal." *Frontiers in Ecology and Evolution* vol. 9,765488 (2021): 1–17. doi:10.3389/fevo.2021.765488.

Shankar Narayan, "Salmon Circle the RAS Tank until Reaching Market Weight": The quotation from Becca Franks is from an article by Ellen Ruppel Shell, originally published as "Bold Experiments in Fish Farming," *Scientific American* 326, 5, 44–57 (May 2022). doi:10.1038/scientificamerican0522-44. The online version, titled "Innovative Fish Farms Aim to Feed the Planet, Save Jobs and Clean Up an

Industry's Dirty Reputation," is at www.scientificamerican.com/article/innovative-fish-farms-aim-to-feed-the-planet-save-jobs-and-clean-up-an-industrys-dirty-reputation/.

Charles Patterson, "Tin Rock at Taylor Dock": The tin rock is a pile of tin scraps that were dumped into Bellingham Bay by the tin-can manufacturer Pacific Steel Works. A nearby placard reads, "The 27 million cans made in 1899 could not fill the demand for cans by Puget Sound salmon packing plants."

Kate Reavey, "feathers of a jay": This poem was published in 2018 in a set of broadsides for the *Tiny Life* project in collaboration with photographer Laura Alisanne.

Judith Roche, "Salmon Suite": The epigraphs for "The River Dance" and "Ghost Salmon" are from *Salmon Coming Home in Search of Sacred Bliss,* Mieko Chikappu, translated from the Ainu by Jane Corddry Langill with Rie Taki and Judith Roche.

Roche's collection *Wisdom of the Body* includes this note: "The Ainu of Northern Japan call salmon 'fish of the gods.' Northwest Pacific Coast First People say, 'the holy fish.' For the Irish, salmon is 'the fish of Wisdom.'"

This series depicts the five species of salmon found in the Northwest. The poems were written as part of the Seattle Arts Commission's 2001 Salmon in the City project, whose aim was to raise public awareness that in 1999, Puget Sound's Chinook salmon were added to the list of "regionally threatened" species under the US Endangered Species Act. A printed version of the poems was designed by Barbara Longo and displayed at the Hiram Chittenden Locks in Seattle's historic Ballard district, the gateway to the Seattle watershed. Constructed by the US Army Corps of Engineers in 1917, the Locks include a fish ladder for migrating salmon.

Joan Roger, "Cento for the Salmon": Sources for the lines in this cento: "So early it's still almost dark out," Raymond Carver, "Happiness"; "A wind from the pine-trees trickles on my bare head," Li Po, "In the Mountains on a Summer Day"; "I am just a shadow," Hafiz, "Infinite Incandescence"; "In the eddies of the water," Linda Hogan, "Song for the Turtles in the Gulf"; "And I am ready like the young salmon," David Whyte, "A Song for the Salmon"; "In shade, beneath hidden stars," Laura Foley, "The Once Invisible Garden"; "At the source of the longest river," T.S. Eliot, "Little Gidding"; "The birds have quieted in the forest," Johann Wolfgang von Goethe, "Wanderer's Night Song"; "And I lift them," Pesha Joyce Gertler, "The Healing Time"; "And that too is more than enough," Jack Gilbert, "The Lost Hotels of Paris"; "If only I could look beneath my skin," James Crews, "The Body Electric"; "As if death were nowhere," Li-Young Lee, "From Blossoms"; "Feel the of water," Jane Hirshfield, "The Supple Deer"; "This is a special way of being afraid," Philip Larkin, "Aubade"; "Go back into your mist," Primo Levi, "The Surivor"; "Beyond this place of wrath and tears," William Ernest Henley, "Invictus"; "Past the strip malls and the power plants," Ada Limón, "Drowning Creek"; "Past the near meadow, over the still stream," John Keats, "Ode to a Nightingale"; "Open your eyes to water," Lucille Clifton, "Blessing of the Boats"; "It is still a beautiful world," Max Ehrmann, "Desiderata"; "Even when I am no one," David St. John, "In the High Country"; "Remember the sky that you were born under," Joy Harjo, "Remember"; "At the ragged edge of the tree line, sheltered by conifer and bay," Danusha Laméris, "Stone"; "It is time for us to wake," Joyce Sidman, "Starting Now"; "For too many nights now I have not imagined the salmon," David Whyte, "A Song for the Salmon"; "We had been together so very long," Linda Hogan, "Song for the Turtles in the Gulf"; "The course of the river changed," Camille T. Dungy, "Trophic Cascade"; "But that did not keep me from crossing," Billy Collins, "The Lanyard"; "I begin again with the smallest numbers," Naomi Shihab Nye, "Burning the Old Year"; "To start. That's everything we require to keep going," Alberto Ríos, "A House Called Tomorrow"; "To learn the song the first one laid down," Linda Hogan, "After Silence: Return."

Caitlin Scarano, "Newhalem, Late October": The italicized lines are from a quotation by Scott Schuyler in "Controversy Continues between Seattle, Tribes over Skagit River Dam," Kimberly Cauvel, *Skagit Valley Herald*, August 15, 2021, www.goskagit.com/news/environment/controversy-continues-between-seattle-tribes-over-skagit-river-dam/article_e6eaf33f-d50c-539e-98df-5c28c5ad2865.html.

Earle Thompson, "Vigil": Celilo Falls on the Columbia River was an important ancient fishing ground for Indigenous people from all over the Northwest. They continued to fish and hold ceremonial gatherings until the falls were completely covered by a dam constructed in 1956 by the Army Corps of Engineers.

Contributors

Tele Aadsen is a writer, commercial fisherman, fishmonger, and lapsed social worker. She lives ocean-summers as a thankful guest on the waters of Lingít Aaní, Southeast Alaska, aboard the F/V *Nerka* with partner Joel Brady-Power, and land-winters in the Coast Salish territory of Bow, Washington. She self-markets their catch through Nerka Sea-Frozen Salmon, performs annually at Oregon's FisherPoets Gathering, and has a collection of essays forthcoming from Empty Bowl Press in 2023.

Kelli Russell Agodon's newest book, *Dialogues with Rising Tides* (Copper Canyon Press), was a finalist for the Washington State Book Award. She's the cofounder of Two Sylvias Press, where she works as an editor. An avid paddleboarder and hiker, Kelli lives in a rural seaside community on traditional lands of the Chemakum, Coast Salish, S'Klallam, and Suquamish people. Kelli teaches at Pacific Lutheran University's low-residency MFA program, the Rainier Writing Workshop, and is part of Writing the Land, a project between local land trusts and artists to help raise awareness for the preservation of land, ecosystems, and biodiversity. www.agodon.com.

Eileyah Ahmad is a first grader who is a resident of Bothell. She likes writing poems inspired from nature, family, and her life. She performed her most recent poem at Northshore Speaks. The poem was about her grandfather who passed away before she was born.

Luther Allen writes poems and designs buildings in Sumas Mountain, Washington. He cofacilitates the SpeakEasy reading series, is coeditor of *Noisy Water: Poetry from Whatcom County, Washington,* and is the author of a collection of 365 poems, *The View from Lummi Island,* available at http://othermindpress.wordpress.com. His work is included in numerous journals and anthologies, including *WA 129, Refugium: Poems for the Pacific, For Love of Orcas, Washington Poetic Routes,* and *The Madrona Project: Human Communities in Wild Places.* His short story "The Stilled Ring" was a finalist in an annual fiction contest at *Terrain.org.* He views writing as his spiritual practice.

Jane Alynn is a poet and photographic artist. She is the author of the full-length collection *Necessity of Flight* (Cherry Grove, 2011) and a chapbook, *Threads & Dust* (Finishing Line Press, 2005). Her most recent award was second place in *New South's* 2012 poetry contest. Her poems have appeared in numerous journals and anthologies, and those written in collaboration with visual artists have been exhibited in galleries.

Em Arata-Berkel was born and raised in Austin, the weird blue heart of Texas. They made the trek out west to complete a master's in library and information science at the University of Washington, and charmed by the PNW's sublime gloom, they've since put down roots in the greater Seattle area. Em has written creatively since they were knee-high, hiked before they could walk, and delights in excavating information rabbit holes. They enjoy cooking almost as much as eating the results.

Dotty Armstrong lives in Naches, where the sun shines nearly every day. In 2020, the Yakima Coffeehouse Poets published her chapbook *The Book of Common Poems*. In 2019, she won first prize for adult poetry in the Cowiche Canyon Conservancy Nature's Storytellers contest. Her poems have been published widely in local journals. Ever since she was a kid, she has made things, including poetry. She looks closely at ordinary life and writes about it. Her interests include traveling, gardening, hiking, and playing with other people's pets as well as her own. She is still making things.

Gabrielle Bates is the author of *Judas Goat* (Tin House, 2023). Originally from Birmingham, Alabama, she currently lives in Seattle, where she works for Open Books: A Poem Emporium and cohosts the podcast *The Poet Salon*. She is a Ruth Lilly and Dorothy Sargent Rosenberg Poetry Fellowship finalist, and her poems have appeared in *The New Yorker*, the Academy of American Poets Poem-a-Day, *BAX: Best American Experimental Poetry*, and *Ploughshares*, among other journals and anthologies. On Twitter (@GabrielleBates).

Molly Beck: Although poetry was my "mother tongue," I earned a living as a consulting arborist in the Seattle area. I had published a number of poems in small poetry journals prior to returning to school, this time in forest resources. It's been an interesting collage, this synthesis of art and science. I was the only student in Forest Entomology who sensed the irony and pathos in the life cycle of the female scale. It would be another twenty years before I wrote creatively, but subconsciously I was collecting material. Sense of place and the forces of nature are my primary muses.

Scott Bentley (he/they) received a master of fine arts in creative writing and poetics at the University of Washington, Bothell. He's been a curator of the Gamut literary series, a Mineral School resident, a Hugo House Fellow, and an editor at *Clamor*, *Ghost Town*, and *Pacific Review*. His writing and art have appeared in *Breathe*, *Paperbark*, *Abalone Mountain Press*, and elsewhere.

David Berger is an author, poet, and haiku poet. He likes to hike and fish and is a visual artist. His published books include *Razor Clams: Buried Treasure of the Pacific Northwest* (University of Washington Press) and *Bette Alexander: The Music in Us* (Chin Music Press). He wrote about salmon in *About Place Journal*, the literary journal of the Black Earth Institute (http://aboutplacejournal.org/issues/a-river-runs-through-us/contents/david-burger/), and his salmon-related artwork helped celebrate removal of the Elwha dams. His haiku poems have appeared in *First Frost* and other publications. He was an arts critic at the *Seattle Times* and executive director of a botanical garden.

James Bertolino's poetry has received recognition through a Book-of-the-Month Club Poetry Fellowship, the Discovery Award, a National Endowment for the Arts fellowship, the 1996 International Merit Award in Poetry from the *Atlanta Review,* two Quarterly Review of Literature book awards, and the Jeanne Lohmann Poetry Prize for Washington State poets. At eighty years old, he continues to spend time writing poetry and reading other poets' works every single day.

Gloria Bird is a member of the Spokane Tribe and grew up on the Colville and Spokane Reservations in eastern Washington. She received a BA from Lewis & Clark College in 1990 and an MA from the University of Arizona in 1992. Bird is the author of *The River of History* (Trask House Books, 1997) and *Full Moon on the Reservation* (Greenfield Review Press, 1993), which received the Diane Decorah Memorial Award for Poetry. With Joy Harjo, she edited *Reinventing the Enemy's Language: Contemporary Native Women's Writings of North America* (W.W. Norton, 1998). She lives in Spokane.

Judy Blanco and **Lauren Urgenson** work on salmon recovery in King County, Washington. This is their first poem.

Michele Bombardier's debut collection, *What We Do,* was a Washington State Book Award finalist. She is the founder of Fishplate Poetry, which offers workshops and retreats while raising money for humanitarian aid, specifically medical care for refugees. She has published nearly a hundred poems and reviews in journals including *JAMA, Alaska Quarterly Review, Bellevue Literary Review, Parabola,* and others. She has received residencies at Hedgebrook and the Mineral School. Michele is the inaugural poet laureate of Bainbridge Island, where she lives and works.

Karen Bonaudi lives in the Seattle suburbs. She has taught adult and K–12 writing classes, conducted workshops, served as president of the Washington Poets Association, and was instrumental in establishing the poet laureate position in Washington State. Her publishing history includes *Bellingham Review, Pontoon, Cascade Journal, South Dakota Review,* and others. Her poem "Exiles" appeared in *Take a Stand: Art Against Hate* from Raven Chronicles. Her chapbook *Editing a Vapor Trail* was published as part of the Pudding House Press chapbook series.

In third grade, **Elaine Miller Bond** wrote a sparkly little poem about holiday lights that was published in the *Oakland Tribune.* She went on to become senior science writer for the University of California Natural Reserve System. She also wrote and photographed the children's books *Running Wild, Living Wild,* and *Wild Colors of the West.* Bond is photographer for *The Utah Prairie Dog* and author of *The Pupfish Hero* (forthcoming). Her photos have aired on Discovery Channel Canada, and her publishing credits include *Science, Scholastic* (Clifford), *Bay Nature,* and *Fire and Rain: Ecopoetry of California.* Bellingham is her new home. www.elainemillerbond.com.

Andrew Brett: I am a high school student in the Pacific Northwest. I look forward to crunching numbers for a living someday. For fun I compose digital music and write songs that I sing and post to social media. My style is dressing and living outside the box.

Ronda Piszk Broatch is the author of *Lake of Fallen Constellations* (MoonPath Press, 2015) and *Chaos Theory for Beginners* (MoonPath Press, 2023). She is the recipient of an Artist Trust GAP grant. Ronda's journal publications include *Fugue, Blackbird, 2River, Sycamore Review, The Missouri Review, Palette Poetry,* and NPR News/KUOW's *All Things Considered.* She is a graduate student working toward her MFA at Pacific Lutheran University's Rainier Writing Workshop. Ronda lives in Kingston, situated on Suquamish and Port Gamble S'Klallam tribal land.

Informed by extensive studies in the earth sciences and feminist theology, **Jerry Bryan** coordinated fish and watershed restoration and carbon emission reduction projects for forty years, converting antiquated water conveyance infrastructure to state-of-the-art systems that benefit both Pacific salmon and local communities. Throughout his career, Jerry worked to cultivate regenerative practices that seek to empower people to live simply for the common good of all cultures.

Catherine Bull's poems have been published in *FIELD, Literary Bohemian, Unlost Journal, The Operating System, WA 129,* and others. She holds degrees from Oberlin College and UC Davis and lives in Tacoma.

petro c. k. is a temporal being living in the northern limits of Seattle. His creative life has recently included writing, with haiku and other short-form poetry already published or accepted for future publication in over a dozen journals, including *Modern Haiku, Kingfisher, Otoliths,* and *Akitsu Quarterly.* He is working on his first collection of haiku, but he also just got his first kayak, so it may take a little longer now.

Nancy Canyon, NatureCulture's 2023 Writing the Land poet, collaborates with Whatcom Land Trust to write poems about her adopted parcel, Todd Creek. She also works as a writing coach for The Narrative Project, guiding authors through the first draft of a memoir. Nancy paints in an 1898 studio overlooking Bellingham Bay in historic Fairhaven. Her poetry, prose, and art are published in *The Madrona Project: Human Communities in Wild Places, Raven Chronicles, World Enough Writers* anthologies, *Floating Bridge Review,* and *Water~Stone Review,* to name a few. Her novel *Celia's Heaven* and her collection *Saltwater: Poems* are available at villagebooks.com. More at www.nancycanyon.com.

Pamela Hobart Carter is the author of *Her Imaginary Museum* (Kelsay Books), *Held Together with Tape and Glue* (Finishing Line Press), and *Only Connect* (forthcoming from ShabdAaweg). A Slapering Hol Press Chapbook Competition finalist and Pushcart Prize nominee, Carter is coauthor, with Arleen Williams, of twelve short books in easy

English for adults (No Talking Dogs Press). Her plays have been read and produced in Montreal (where she grew up), Seattle (where she lives), and Fort Worth. For more than three decades, Carter was a teacher. A COVID-times activity: adding make-a-poem-at-home lessons to her website: https://playwrightpam.wordpress.com/.

Raymond Carver was born in the logging town of Clatskanie, Oregon, and grew up in Yakima. Carver studied with John Gardner at Chico State, earned his BA from Humboldt State College, and then went on to attend the Iowa Writers' Workshop. Returning to the Northwest, he wrote and eventually published acclaimed short-story collections, including *Will You Please Be Quiet, Please?* (1976), *What We Talk About When We Talk About Love* (1981), and *Cathedral* (1983). A collection of poetry, *A New Path to the Waterfall* (1989), was published posthumously. From the late 1970s until his death, Carver lived with and was married to the poet Tess Gallagher.

Susan Chase-Foster pens poemoirs, prose, and fiction in Raven's Roost, her writing cottage in Bellingham. Her work has appeared in *Cirque, Alaska Women Speak, Heron Clan,* and other publications. She is the author of *Xiexie Taipei,* a collection of poems and photos from Taiwan, and coeditor of *This Uncommon Solitude: Pandemic Poetry from the Pacific Northwest.* Susan is currently dividing her time between wrapping up a novel set in a fishing village on the west coast of Mexico and gathering her interior Alaska writings into a volume. Her blog hibernates at stilllifewithtortillas.com.

Joanne Clarkson's sixth poetry collection, *Hospice House,* was accepted by MoonPath Press and will appear in 2023. Her poems have been published in such journals as *Poetry Northwest, Nimrod, Poet Lore, Western Humanities Review,* and *Beloit Poetry Journal.* She has received an Artist Trust grant and an NEH grant to teach poetry in rural libraries. Clarkson has master's degrees in English and library science and has taught and worked for many years as a professional librarian. After caring for her mother through a long illness, she recareered as a registered nurse working in home health and hospice. See more at http://joanneclarkson.com.

Finn Coffin is a mostly real person from a small town in southern Washington called White Salmon. I spend my summers there where I work on an excellent catering crew as a server and occasional salmon-prepper. The other three seasons I spend in Bellingham where I study geology at Western Washington University. I like to spend most of my time in the rocks—climbing, collecting, and ogling. I also enjoy thoughtful and balanced food as well as honest and simple writing. Though I'm an avid reader, I have yet to nail down this whole writing thing.

Linda Conroy, a Bellingham resident and retired social worker, likes to write about the complexity of human behavior and the connection between human nature and the natural world through the changing times, reflecting on what she sees and hears. She enjoys a daily writing practice and supports friends in their writing efforts. Her poetry has appeared in various journals and anthologies. She is the author of a poetry collection, *Ordinary Signs.* Her second book, *Familiar Sky,* was published in the fall of 2022.

Catherine Crawford has written all her life and brings to her work a background in business, academic, and fine-arts writing. She has made her living teaching writing at the four-year-college-degree level and creating training materials for the electronics industry. Catherine cherishes the natural world, listening to it and spending time outdoors. Her father taught her to fish in Wisconsin's Northwoods, traditional home of the Menominee Indians. She still enjoys casting lines in the water and describes herself as a green writer.

Laura Da' is the author of *Tributaries,* winner of the American Book Award, and *Instruments of the True Measure,* winner of the Washington State Book Award. Da' is Eastern Shawnee. She studied creative writing at the University of Washington and the Institute of American Indian Arts. A lifetime resident of the Pacific Northwest, Da' was writer-in-residence for Richard Hugo House and is the current poet laureate for the City of Redmond.

Fig DePaolo was born in 2005 in Spokane. He is a poet and writer obsessed with gestures, touch, nature, gender, and intertextuality. He has an orange tabby cat who is often near when he writes.

Alice Derry is the author of six volumes of poetry, most recently *Asking* (MoonPath Press, 2022), and three chapbooks, including translations of poems by Rainer Rilke. She taught for thirty years at Peninsula College, where she curated the Foothills Poetry Series. Since retirement, she has helped local tribal members access poetry. Raymond Carver chose her first poetry manuscript, *Stages of Twilight,* for the King County Arts Prize. *Strangers to Their Courage* was a finalist for the Washington State Book Award. She lives and works on Washington's Olympic Peninsula. www.alicederry.com.

Randall Dills is a former academic and day laborer who now lives in a small cottage on a wooded farm on Fidalgo Island in Washington State on land belonging to the Swinomish Indian Tribal Community. For many years I wrote only in my journal, but now I seek community with other poets and readers. My poems have appeared in the *Eastern Iowa Review* and *Cirque.* FutureCycle Press will publish my first book in February 2023.

Patrick Dixon is retired from careers in teaching and commercial fishing. A past member of the Olympia Poetry Network board of directors, he has been published in *Cirque, Oberon, The Raven Chronicles,* and *The Tishman Review.* His work has appeared in the anthologies *FISH 2015, WA 129,* and *Take a Stand: Art Against Hate,* the Washington State Book Award–winning anthology from Raven Chronicles Press. He received an

Artist Trust grant to edit *Anchored in Deep Water: The FisherPoets Anthology* (2014). His chapbook *Arc of Visibility* won the 2015 Alabama State Poetry Society's Morris Memorial Award. He lives in Olympia.

Victoria Doerper writes poetry and creative nonfiction from her cottage near the shore of the Salish Sea. Inspired by the natural things of this world, her poems examine love, loss, and wonder. Her work appears in several literary publications, including *Cirque; Noisy Water: Poetry from Whatcom County, Washington; Bindweed; Front Porch Review;* and *The Plum Tree Tavern,* as well as *Orion* magazine. Her book of poems, *What If We All Bloomed?: Poems of Nature, Love, and Aging,* was published by Penchant Press in 2019.

Peter Donaldson is a strategic storyteller with forty years of experience in playwriting, poetry, public speaking, curriculum design, and community facilitation. He is director of learning for Sustainability Ambassadors, coaching students, teachers, and community leaders on impact strategies for city climate action plans. Recognized as National Youth Theater Director of the Year in 1994, Peter also wrote and acted in his own one-man touring shows, *Leonardo da Vinci* and *Salmonpeople,* with follow-up seminars at high schools across the Northwest. In 2009, he was appointed distinguished scholar at The Evergreen State College, where he facilitated seminars on creativity and systems thinking.

Alex C. Eisenberg is a child of the western high desert and the Pacific Northwest rainforest, with ancestral ties to Eastern Europe. Her soul is rooted in these wonderful landscapes, and her writing springs forth from that connection. Alex currently lives by candlelight with her beloved cat in the foothills of the Olympic Mountains. Her poems have been featured in *About Place Journal, River Heron Review, Pangyrus Lit, The Shore,* and others. To read her published works, visit alexandriaceisenberg.wordpress.com. You can find her @alexceisenberg on Twitter.

Katy E. Ellis grew up under evergreens, alders, a messy cottonwood, and high-voltage powerlines in Renton, Washington, which is the ancestral home of the Duwamish people. She is the author of the novel-length prose poem *Home Water, Home Land* (Tolsun Books) and three chapbooks, including *Night Watch,* winner of the 2017 Floating Bridge Press chapbook competition. Her poetry and short fiction have appeared in *Pithead Chapel, Rise Up, The American Journal of Poetry, Literary Mama, MAYDAY, CALYX: A Journal of Art and Literature by Women, Burnside Review,* and in the Canadian journals *PRISM International, Grain,* and *Fiddlehead.*

Gary Evans learned of haiku while taking a class in world literature in high school. Encouraged by his teacher to write a few poems of his own, Gary's first published haiku appeared in *Haiku Highlights* in 1967. After a career in education, he returned to his interest in Japanese poetry forms, including haiku, haibun, photo haiga, and rengay. His poetry has been published in *The Heron's Nest, Mariposa, Acorn, Modern Haiku, Frogpond,* and *Bottle Rockets,* among others. His and fellow haiku author Seren Fargo's rengay was selected for first place in the 2017 Haiku Poets of Northern California annual rengay competition.

Scott Ferry helps our veterans heal as an RN in the Seattle area. His work has been published in journals such as *New York Quarterly, The Night Heron Barks,* and *Banyan.* He has authored seven books of poetry, the most recent being *The Long Blade of Days Ahead* from Impspired Press. More of his work can be found at ferrypoetry.com.

Kathleen Flenniken is the author of three poetry collections, most recently *Post Romantic* (Pacific Northwest Poetry Series, 2020), a finalist for the Washington State Book Award. *Plume* (2012), a personal history in poems about the Hanford Nuclear Site, won the Washington State Book Award and was a finalist for the Poetry Society of America's William Carlos Williams Award. Her first book, *Famous* (2006), won the Prairie Schooner Book Prize in Poetry and was named a notable book by the National Library Association. Kathleen served as the Washington State Poet Laureate from 2012 to 2014.

Gabriela Denise Frank is a transdisciplinary storyteller, editor, and educator living in the Pacific Northwest. Her work has appeared in *True Story, HAD, Hunger Mountain, DIAGRAM, The Bureau Dispatch, Baltimore Review, The Normal School, The Rumpus,* and elsewhere. The author of *Pity She Didn't Stay 'Til the End* (Bottlecap Press), she serves as the creative nonfiction editor of *Crab Creek Review.* www.gabrieladenisefrank.com.

Tess Gallagher's eleventh volume of poetry, *Is, Is Not,* was published in May 2019 by Graywolf Press. *Midnight Lantern: New and Selected Poems* is the most comprehensive offering of her poems. Other poetry includes *Dear Ghosts* and *Moon Crossing Bridge.* Gallagher's *The Man from Kinvara: Selected Stories* is the basis for film episodes under development. She divides her time between her hometown of Port Angeles, Washington, and her cottage in the west of Ireland. She is the literary executor of her late husband, Raymond Carver, and will be the inaugural writer-in-residence for Port Angeles's state-of-the-art Field Arts and Events Hall.

Sierra Golden's debut collection, *The Slow Art,* was published by Bear Star Press and was a finalist for the 2019 Washington State Book Award. Golden's poems appear in literary journals such as *Prairie Schooner, Permafrost,* and *Ploughshares.* She currently lives in eastern Washington with her partner and young son and works as the associate director of the nonprofit TwispWorks.

Originally from New York, **Seth Goldstein** has lived in Olympia for close to two decades. He is a congregational rabbi, and in that capacity he is committed to both creating vibrant spiritual community and bringing a spiritual voice to issues of social justice and common concern. He also finds inspiration in the natural world, particularly in the Pacific Northwest. Long a reader of poetry, he is new to writing. The poem in this anthology is inspired by the intersection of the fall salmon run and the Jewish High Holidays, the most sacred time on the Jewish calendar.

Meagan Graves is a writer from Portland, Oregon, and is the recipient of the 2022 Michael and Gail Gurian Writing Award for poetry. Through poetry, prose, and playwriting, she explores the themes of home and connection. Meagan is currently completing a degree in English and communication studies at Gonzaga University.

John S Green, author of *Whimsy Park: Children's Poems for the Whole Family,* is widely published in all styles of poetry—especially haiku. John lived in Europe before moving to the United States at age thirteen. His daughter cooks with spice, and his wife still laughs at his jokes.

Amy Gulick is a writer and photographer and the author of *The Salmon Way: An Alaska State of Mind* and *Salmon in the Trees: Life in Alaska's Tongass Rain Forest.* Her stories and images have appeared in *Smithsonian, Audubon, National Wildlife,* and other publications. She is the recipient of the Voices of the Wild Award from the Alaska Wilderness League, the Conservation Voices Award from Washington Wild, and a Lowell Thomas Award from the Society of American Travel Writers Foundation. She is a fellow of the Safina Center. See more of her work at amygulick.com.

Chris Gusta is a teacher and writer living in Bellingham. Former editor of *Your Hands, Your Mouth* magazine, he has a book coming out this year from Really Serious Lit called *The Air Is Smokey Because We Don't Love Each Other Enough.* He's doing okay.

Tom Hahney: Not much to say: a seventy-nine-year-old former instructor pilot, engineer, architect, and therapist; current husband, father, grandpa, meditator, yogi. Enjoys reading poetry, especially haiku.

Ed Harkness: I live about a mile from where I grew up, in the Haller Lake neighborhood of north Seattle. BA, University of Washington; MFA, University of Montana. My second great-grandfather, a Quebecois named Moses Graff, married a Haida woman, Mary Cabana, in Seattle in 1866. Sophia Graff, my great-grandmother, was born in the vicinity of Alki Point in 1870. I fell into poetry by accident when, as a student at the UW, I attended a reading by a poet named Richard Hugo. His voice, his words, made my neck hairs stand on end.

Barbara Hersey: My first poems were haiku, written for a high school English assignment in 1964. Haiku remains one of my favorite forms. I was born and raised in Wenatchee, and the spirit of Nch'i-Wàna (the Columbia) flows through my veins, as it does everyone's living near that great river. Unfortunately, I grew up celebrating the power created by dams more than salmon. Many influences have given me a different perspective.

Alicia Hokanson's first collection of poems, *Mapping the Distance,* was selected by Carolyn Kizer for the King County Arts Commission publication prize. Two chapbooks, *Phosphorous* and *Insistent in the Skin,* were published by Brooding Heron Press. Her newest collection, *Perishable World,* was released by Pleasure Boat Studio in the summer of 2021 and awarded the Eyelands Book Award grand prize for poetry in December 2021. She lives in Seattle in the Piper's Creek watershed, where the salmon return to the creek each autumn. She also spends time on Waldron Island in the Salish Sea.

Ann Batchelor Hursey's poems have appeared on Seattle buses, in *The Seattle Review,* and in *Crab Creek Review,* among other places. Her poetry collection *A Certain Hold* was published by Finishing Line Press in 2014. Ann has been awarded writing residencies with Jack Straw Writers, Hypatia-in-the-Woods, and Soapstone: A Writing Retreat for Women. Her most recent book, *Field Notes to Maya Lin's Confluence Project Landscapes,* a hybrid collection of prose and poems, was published by Salmonberry Press in 2021. Ann received her MFA from the Rainier Writing Workshop at Pacific Lutheran University. Born in northeast Ohio, Ann now calls the Pacific Northwest home.

Beverly Anne Jackson was born in Detroit in 1946 and grew up in neighboring Dearborn. I graduated from the University of Michigan in 1969. Highlights included attending a Robert Frost poetry reading and having Donald Hall as poetry professor. I am an amateur poetry and haiku writer. I've won a few competitions with my poems. My husband and I post a monthly gnome email with photo and haiku. When I moved to Washington, I was astounded by Nature's grandeur here. I first witnessed returning salmon at Tumwater Falls Park and became enthralled. Each fall, I pay my respects to them.

Christopher J. Jarmick was once an LA-based TV producer/screenwriter. He's curated/hosted monthly poetry readings and special events in the Pacific Northwest since 2001. In 2016, Chris became the owner of BookTree, Kirkland, Washington's only new and gently used independent bookstore (www.booktreekirkland.com/). His latest poetry collection, *Not Aloud* (2015), is from MoonPath Press. Other books include *Ignition* (2008) and the mystery-thriller *The Glass Cocoon* (2001). His work has appeared in newspapers, magazines, journals, online, and in anthologies such as *Footbridge Above the Falls* (Rose Alley Press, 2019).

Tom Jay was born in Manhattan, Kansas, in 1943. An active member of the Northwest art community since 1966, he built the first bronze-casting facility for Seattle University and supervised construction of casting facilities at the University of Washington. Receiving an MFA from the University of Washington in 1969, he established Riverdog

Fine Arts Foundry, which cast his own work and that of sculptors throughout the Northwest. He and his wife, Sara Mall Johani, engaged the community imagination in place-based culture through art, festivals, and salmon-restoration projects. His essays and poems were collected in *The Blossoms Are Ghosts at the Wedding.* A revised and expanded edition was published by Empty Bowl Press in 2019, the year Tom died.

Georgia Johnson has made a living baking, chefing, meddling, writing, and teaching. She has called the Skagit Valley home for thirty-five years. She recently moved to a small farm on Fidalgo Island with her husband and critters, where poems are grown. Desert Rose Press published a chapbook, *Finding Beet Seed,* in 2000, made with two other artists, Clifford Burke and Maggie Wilder. In 2017, Flying Trout Press, Bellingham, published *Just Past Dew Point.* Georgia has been involved with the Skagit River Poetry Foundation board since its inception in 1998.

Jill McCabe Johnson is the author of the poetry collections *Revolutions We'd Hoped We'd Outgrown,* shortlisted for Jane's Stories Press Foundation's Clara Johnson Award in Women's Literature, and *Diary of the One Swelling Sea,* winner of a Nautilus Silver Award in Poetry, plus the chapbooks *Pendulum* and *Borderlines.* Recent works have appeared in *Slate, Fourth Genre, Waxwing, Terrain.org, Brevity,* and *Crab Creek Review.* Jill is the founder of Wandering Aengus Press and makes her home on an island in the Salish Sea.

Tegan Keyes is a senior at Western Washington University pursuing a degree in environmental studies and writing poems in her spare time. She loves the Salish Sea and is endlessly grateful to live in such a complex and beautiful area.

Shelley Kirk-Rudeen developed the trail guide program for the Kennedy Creek Salmon Trail in southern Puget Sound and managed the trail for five years. She created salmon and salmon habitat–related interpretive signage and other outreach materials for the US Forest Service Methow Ranger District's Respect the River program. Her poems have appeared in several journals and anthologies and in *WA 129.* Shelley has self-published two volumes of poetry. Now retired, she lives in Olympia and loves sharing the natural world with her husband and four young grandsons.

Catherine Kyle is the author of *Fulgurite* (Cornerstone Press, forthcoming), *Shelter in Place* (Spuyten Duyvil, 2019), and other poetry collections. Her writing has appeared in *Bellingham Review, Colorado Review, Mid-American Review,* and other journals, and has been honored by the Idaho Commission on the Arts, the Alexa Rose Foundation, and other organizations. She was the winner of the 2019–2020 COG Poetry Award, a finalist for the 2021 Mississippi Review Prize in poetry, and a finalist for the 2021 Pinch Literary Awards. She is an assistant professor at DigiPen Institute of Technology, where she teaches creative writing.

Linda Quinby Lambert lives in Bellingham. She is the mother of four sons and three daughters. A retired academic library director, she has fun working as ghostwriter of memoirs. She is a member of Poetry Club, led by Dr. Ron Leatherbarrow and Shannon Law; Red Wheelbarrow Writers; two writing critique groups; two book clubs; and the League of Women Voters. She holds degrees in journalism (MA, University of Southern California), library science (MLS, Emporia State University), and creative writing (MFA, University of Southern Maine).

Susan Landgraf was awarded an Academy of American Poets Laureate Fellowship in 2020. The resulting book of Muckleshoot Indian Tribe poetry will be published by Washington State University Press. Her books include *The Inspired Poet,* a writing exercise book from Two Sylvias Press (2019); *What We Bury Changes the Ground;* and a chapbook, *Other Voices.* More than four hundred of Susan's poems have appeared in publications such as *Prairie Schooner, Poet Lore, Margie, Nimrod, The Meadow, Rattle,* and *CALYX.* Her chapbook is forthcoming from Ravenna Press. She served as poet laureate of Auburn, Washington, from 2018 to 2020.

Sasha taqwšəblu LaPointe is from the Upper Skagit and Nooksack Indian Tribes. She holds a double MFA from the Institute of American Indian Arts in creative nonfiction and poetry. Her memoir, *Red Paint,* is available through Counterpoint Press. Her collection of poetry, *Rose Quartz,* is forthcoming from Milkweed in 2023.

Cathy Lear's first taste of salmon—freshly caught sockeye from the waters of Alaska—opened her eyes and heart to the wonders of these amazing fish. Since that time, she has worked to restore their habitat on the north Olympic Peninsula of Washington State. Her current efforts include reconnecting the lower Dungeness River to more than one hundred acres of its floodplain.

Rob Lewis is a poet, activist, and housepainter. His writings have been published in *Dark Mountain, Counterflow, Manzanita, Atlanta Review, The Southern Review, Cascadia Daily, For the Love of Orcas,* and others. As owner of Earth Craft Painting, he also works to revive the use of local wild clays to paint our work and living spaces.

Paul Lindholdt: A native Washingtonian, I began work as a longshoreman and Teamster in Bellingham and Seattle. After earning the PhD back east, I am grateful to be home. Grateful also to cherish the teaching, the students that make classes so rewarding, and the support for public writing. As a writer I am interested chiefly in the environmental humanities, and particularly in how creative writing and culture studies may nourish one another.

Deirdre Lockwood is a poet and fiction writer based in Seattle. Her poems have appeared in *Poetry Northwest, The Threepenny Review, The Yale Review,* and elsewhere. She has received support from the Fulbright program, Hugo House, the Elizabeth

George Foundation, Artist Trust, Marble House Project, Willapa Bay AiR, and the Sitka Center for Art and Ecology, and is working on a novel. She has an MFA in poetry from Boston University and a PhD in oceanography from the University of Washington. Find her at deirdrelockwood.com and on Twitter @deirdrelockwood.

Priscilla Long is the author of two books of poems, *Holy Magic* (MoonPath Press) and *Crossing Over* (University of New Mexico Press). Her latest book, on thriving in old age, is *Dancing with the Muse in Old Age* (Coffeetown Press). She is a longtime independent teacher of writing (her how-to-write book is *The Writer's Portable Mentor*) and a writer of science, creative nonfiction, history, and fiction. She is founding and consulting editor of HistoryLink.org, the free online encyclopedia of Washington State history.

Linera Lucas won the Crucible Fiction Prize. Her poetry has appeared in *The American Journal of Poetry, Briar Cliff Review, Cirque, Eclectica, PageBoy Magazine,* the Museum of Northwest Art's website, *Quartet, Redactions, River Mouth Review, Spillway,* and elsewhere. She is coeditor of *When Home Is Not Safe: Writings on Domestic Abuse,* published by McFarland. Her short stories have been anthologized and recorded for the Jack Straw Talking Chairs project. Lucas has a BA from Reed College and an MFA from Queens University of Charlotte and has taught at the University of Washington Women's Center and at Hugo House. www.lineralucas.com.

M.L. Lyke freelances for the University of Washington and is part of The Washington Post Talent Network. I worked for the *Seattle Post-Intelligencer* for many years, in roles ranging from writing coach to war correspondent. Nominated for a Pulitzer Prize, I have won numerous national awards for writing and editing. My resume includes publication of a serial novel called *Skukum Kilay;* authoring the photo book *Harvesting the Light;* writing *Research That Matters* for the UW; and editing *Medicine and Meditation* and *Black Pearls: An African-American Woman's Guide to Making Smart Love Choices.* I write poetry and fiction for the love of it.

Tara Mesalik MacMahon: I am an emerging poet. My first book of poems, *Barefoot Up the Mountain,* won the 2020 Open Country Press chapbook contest. I am a graduate from Pomona College and Harvard University. My poems appear or are forthcoming in *Jabberwock Review, Nimrod, Poet Lore, Mud Season Review, Rhino,* and Red Hen Press's *New Moons: Contemporary Writing by North American Muslims,* among others. Additional honors and prizes include *Jabberwock's* Editors' Prize, *Dogwood's* Poetry Prize, *Frontier's* Industry Prize, and *Nimrod's* Francine Ringold Award for New Writers. I reside in the San Juan Islands with my husband, Paul, and our rescue dog, Hector.

Carole MacRury resides in Point Roberts, Washington, a unique border town and peninsula on the Salish Sea that inspires her work. Her poems have won awards and been published widely in North American and international journals and anthologies and have been translated into many languages. Her nature photographs have been featured on the covers of numerous poetry journals and anthologies. She is the author of *In the Company of Crows: Haiku and Tanka Between the Tides* (Black Cat Press, 2008; second printing, 2018) and *The Tang of Nasturtiums,* an award-winning e-chapbook (Snapshot Press, 2012).

Linda Malnack is the author of two poetry chapbooks, *21 Boxes* (dancing girl press) and *Bone Beads* (Paper Boat Press). Her poetry has recently appeared in *Prairie Schooner, Cloudbank, The Ilanot Review, Fairy Tale Review, Camas Magazine,* and elsewhere. Linda is an assistant poetry editor for *Crab Creek Review.*

C. R. Manley is a children's book author, technical writer, poet, and geologist. His picture books include *The Summer Nick Taught His Cats to Read* and *Shawn Loves Sharks* (winner of the Washington State Book Award), *The Rescuer of Tiny Creatures* (all fiction), *Just Right: Searching for the Goldilocks Planet* (nonfiction), and *The Crane Girl* (retold folktale). He's also published poetry and prose in *Windfall, Arnazella, Pontoon, Isotope, Paragraph, South Dakota Review, American Mineralogist, Bulletin of Volcanology,* and elsewhere. He knows enough about Mt. Rainier to live beyond its reach, on high ground, in Bellevue.

Alexander A. Manzoni has been writing poetry and prose for over twenty years. In September 2014, after recovering from six years of drug abuse and run-ins with the law, he got clean and moved to Spokane from Newfield, New Jersey. This neurodivergent bipolar writer loves to perform at various events and open mics in the Spokane-C.D.A. area, and currently holds the questionable title of "Spokane's most followed TikTok-based poet." Publishing credits include *The Green Shoe Sanctuary, Verse Virtual, Every Writer's Resource, FIVE Poetry Magazine, In-Parentheses, PicturesofPoets.com, Spokane Writes: A Poetry & Prose Anthology,* and *Washington's Best Emerging Poets 2019.*

Eugene Marckx studied at the University of Washington under Theodore Roethke in the final year of Roethke's life. He spent his employed life working on the floor of a large bakery and raising five children in a marriage that slowly failed. His writing comes from uncomfortable questions he ponders in a men's group—A Gathering of Men—in Snohomish County. He has completed a novel, *Broken Charlie,* about the historic clear-cutting of western forests. Eugene has been featured at open mics. Two of his poems were published in *Terrain.org* and one in a recent anthology of local poets.

Michael Martin used to be a lawyer but left the dark side. He was a public librarian for over fifteen years in Selah, Washington, located in the high shrubsteppe. Now Michael enjoys the wonders of nature and what is to be seen, heard, and smelled, with chickens and a goat outside at home, and cats, lizards, and snakes (and a tarantula) inside the house. Michael occasionally writes haiku or odes to coyotes.

Christen Mattix is the author of the contemplative memoir *Skein: The Heartbreaks and Triumphs of a Long Distance Knitter.* Christen's writing has appeared in *Psalter & Lyre, For Love of Orcas, Clover, A Literary Rag,* and *Seen Journal,* among others. Christen is honored to take part in the Komo Kulshan haiku writing group. Her latest haiku is forthcoming in the October newsletter of the Haiku Society of America. Christen is also a muralist, children's book illustrator, and failed nun, among other titles. christenmattix.com.

Andrew Shattuck McBride grew up in Volcano, Hawai'i, six miles from the summit of Kīlauea volcano. Based now in Washington State, he is coeditor of *For Love of Orcas* (Wandering Aengus, 2019). His work appears or is forthcoming in *Black Horse Review, The Cabinet of Heed, Clockhouse, Crab Creek Review, Empty Mirror, Evening Street Review, Floating Bridge Review, Months to Years, Passager Journal, Pensive: A Global Journal of Spirituality and the Arts,* and *POETiCA REViEW.*

Phelps McIlvaine, sixty-nine, is a retired institutional investment manager. Phelps's family moved to Bellingham in 1994. He is a lifelong fisher, boater, and outdoorsman. Since 1995, Phelps has been an active volunteer, past board president, and past capital campaign chair for the Nooksack Salmon Enhancement Association (NSEA.org). Phelps married Amy Hanna in 1986. They have three children: Hanna is a labor and delivery nurse, Cole is a director at Zillow Corporation, and Ava is a scientist at the Center for Mass Accelerator Spectrometry, Lawrence Livermore National Laboratory. The poem in this collection was written as a nondenominational blessing for meals and gatherings.

Neil McKay grew up near the Duwamish River and Boeing Field in south Seattle. He currently lives in Bellingham and works for the Whatcom County Library System. He has performed as a spoken word poet at the Seattle Poetry Slam and poetry events in Bellingham, Ellensburg, Everett, and Ferndale. He has an MA in strategic communication from Washington State University and has walked on the halo of the Space Needle in Seattle. He is an active fundraiser for Fred Hutchinson Cancer Research Center and an advocate for public libraries and public transportation. He is still learning.

Mary McMinn is a retired English teacher.

K'Ehleyr McNulty (she/they:ella/elle) is a citizen of the Ohlone Costanoan Esselen Nation of what is now known as Carmel Valley and Monterey Bay, California. She is a poet, artist, and scientist currently living on the lands of the Lower Elwha Klallam Tribe. Attending a monthly gathering affectionately dubbed Native Poets, K'Ehleyr writes with, listens to, and learns from friends whose works are eternally inspiring. They are honored to have their poem "Unprecedented" included in *The Madrona Project: Keep a Green Bough: Voices from the Heart of Cascadia,* edited by Holly J. Hughes.

Rainbow Medicine-Walker is an enrolled member of the federally recognized Cherokee Nation. She is the granddaughter of Cherokee Admiral JJ Clark, Chief Water Dweller, and Chief Thunderbird. Rainbow is an Elder, veteran, and Ceremonial Leader. She has written, spoken, and published speeches, articles, essays, and poems emphasizing our essential belonging to Mother Earth, our unbreakable connection to the ancestors, and honoring earth traditions, tribal history, and exposing political agendas.

Maiah A. Merino, a Chicana poet and mixed-genre writer, recently guest coedited *The Yellow Medicine Review*'s Spring 2022 issue, *Miracles & Defining Moments.* She has poems in *In Xóxitl in cuícatl: Flor y Canto, Antología de poesía* and is a 2021–22 Writing the Land poet and recipient of a 2021 Artist Trust GAP award. Her work appears in *The Yellow Medicine Review* and *The Raven Chronicles.* A past writer-in-residence with Seattle Arts & Lectures and Path with Art, Maiah utilizes her training as a narrative therapist and writer to help herself and others navigate and reimagine new stories.

Jory Mickelson is a trans writer whose first book, *Wilderness//Kingdom,* is the inaugural winner of the Evergreen Award Tour from Floating Bridge Press and winner of the 2020 High Plains Book Award in Poetry. Their publications include *Court Green, DIAGRAM, Jubilat, Terrain.org,* and *The Rumpus.* They are the recipient of an Academy of American Poets Prize and were awarded fellowships from the Lambda Literary Foundation, Winter Tangerine, and the Helene Wurlitzer Foundation of New Mexico. They were a 2022 Jack Straw Writer in Seattle.

Audrey Sterud Miller lives on the homelands of her people, the Puyallup Nation. A busy seventh grader, she spends her free time writing poetry and stories, acting in plays, and singing in the shower.

Dian Million (Tanana Athabascan) is an associate professor in the Department of American Indian Studies at the University of Washington in Seattle. She is the author of *Therapeutic Nations: Healing in an Age of Indigenous Human Rights* (University of Arizona Press, Critical Issues in Indigenous Studies Series, 2013). Her poems can be found in *Dancing on the Rim of the World* (Lerner, 1990), *Reinventing the Enemy's Language* (Bird and Harjo, 1997), *When the Light of the World Was Subdued, Our Songs Came Through* (Harjo, 2020), and, most recently, in the volume *Ndè Sı̀ı̀ Wet'aà: Northern Indigenous Voices on Land, Life, & Art* (Sage, Thumlee, Simpson, 2022).

Donald James Mitchell has lived his whole life in Deming, Washington, writing poems in the old-growth Douglas fir and red cedar house his great-grandfather built at the close of the nineteenth century. His self-published books of poetry include *Signs of Faith, The Shark Skin Man, Hello Eternity, No Message, Something Glorious,* and *Strays.* He has also self-published one novel, *ΙΩΝΑΣ.*

Nimisha Mondal is an emerging poet with work previously published in *Courageous Creativity*. She is an experienced stage performer of classical and folk dances and the written word. Born and raised in the Pacific Northwest, she is now raising her own family here, and works by day to advance educational equity for all.

Brad Monsma is the author of *The Sespe Wild: Southern California's Last Free River*, which has a chapter on the remarkable southern steelhead. His essays have appeared in *The Surfer's Journal, High Country News, Kyoto Journal*, various academic journals and anthologies, and *Rites of Green*, the journal of Humanities Washington. With Amiko Matsuo, Monsma translated *Art Place Japan*, a book about the Echigo-Tsumari Art Triennale. They also collaborated on *Pyrometric*, a series of installations and performance pieces about material collaborations with fire, recently published in *Terrain.org*.

Mitzi McMillan Moore is a poet, singer, and teacher. She holds an MA in English from Western Washington University and has lived in the Bellingham area for over thirty years.

AxeS Mundi: A musician, poet, and scholar, with a background in mathematics-economics (BA from Claremont McKenna College), anthropology (MA from The New School for Social Research), and environmental and natural resources law (JD from University of Oregon School of Law), is a member of the American Association for Advancement in Science and has published poems in *The American Poetry Anthology* and *Active Voices Volume 2* from the Osher Lifelong Learning Institute at UCSD. Original recordings (available on iTunes) include CDs titled *SoLAce* and *Orb*. He may be found meandering the meadows of Upper Tallawhalt with faithful feline companion Lady Mosaic.

Born in the Ohio River valley, **Anne Murphy** migrated west to the call of the Pacific and its wildness. A career in nonprofit conservation and education kept her in the milieu of citizen-driven work on the shores and watersheds of the Salish Sea. Since retiring in 2013, she has shifted from technical, persuasive writing to another calling—poetry. She listens for the earth's guidance and tries not to impede its generosity. She lives in traditional Chemakum and S'Klallam territory, along a creek on Washington State's Olympic Peninsula.

Hank Muska is a seventy-one-year-old retired salmon fisherman. All I am can be credited to salmon. I am a man of few words and fewer thoughts.

JS Nahani's passion lies at the intersection of soul-searching, truth-telling, story-weaving, and community-building. She works as a writer, editor, creative coach, group facilitator, and performing artist. She is published in *For Love of Orcas, Psaltery & Lyre, Kumquat Challenge, Yours Truly, Peace Poems Volume III, VoiceCatcher, Poem Booth Bellingham*, and more. Jay uses her MSW and Expressive Arts Therapy training to guide groups and individuals through Creative Insights with Jay; she birthed and facilitates writing groups such as Heart Writers Collective and JUST Write!, focusing on self-awareness, healing, and activism. For more information or to be in touch, visit creativeinsightswithjay.com.

Shankar Narayan explores identity, power, mythology, and technology in a world where the body is flung across borders yet possesses unrivaled power to transcend them. Shankar is a five-time Pushcart Prize nominee and the winner of prizes and fellowships from Kundiman, Hugo House, Jack Straw, *Flyway, River Heron,* and 4Culture. His chapbook *Postcards from the New World* won the Paper Nautilus chapbook prize. He awakens to the wonders of Cascadia every day, but his heart yearns east to his other hometown, Delhi. Connect with him at shankarnarayan.net.

Jon Neher: I am a clinical professor of family medicine at the University of Washington (Seattle), the associate program director at the UW/Valley Family Medicine residency program, and editor-in-chief of the journal *Evidence-Based Practice,* published by the Family Physician's Inquiries Network and Wolters-Kluwer. I live in Renton.

Poet/interviewer **Paul E. Nelson** is the son of a labor activist father and Cuban immigrant mother. A King County resident since 1988, he founded Cascadia Poetics LAB (formerly SPLAB) and the Cascadia Poetry Festival. Since 1993, CPL has produced hundreds of poetry events and seven hundred hours of interviews. Paul's books include *Haibun de la Serna, A Time Before Slaughter/Pig War & Other Songs of Cascadia* (2009), *American Prophets* (interviews 1994–2012), *American Sentences* (2015, 2021), and *Organic in Cascadia: A Sequence of Energies* (2013). He writes an American Sentence every day and lives in Rainier Beach in Cascadia's Cedar River watershed.

Sierra Nelson is a poet, lyric essayist, performance artist, and teacher. Her books include *The Lachrymose Report* (Poetry Northwest Editions), the chapbook *In Case of Loss* (Toadlily Press), and collaborations with artist Loren Erdrich, including *I Take Back the Sponge Cake* (Rose Metal Press) and the artist book *Isolation.* Her poems have appeared in journals and anthologies such as *Narrative, Tin House, Pleiades,* and *Cascadia Field Guide: Art, Ecology, Poetry* and been exhibited in Seattle Metro buses, at the Seattle Aquarium, and in the Slovenian Natural History Museum. She is also president of Seattle's Cephalopod Appreciation Society.

Duane Niatum, Jamestown S'Klallam tribe, writes poems, stories, and essays. His work has been widely published in the US and abroad and translated into fourteen languages. His ninth book of poems is *Earth Vowels* (2017), and his tenth book is *Sea Changes* (2020). He was invited to read his poems at the Library of Congress and the International Poetry Festival in Rotterdam, the Netherlands. His book *Songs for the Harvester of Dreams* won the American Book Award. The Pacific Northwest landscape and legends of his ancestors shape his writings. He received his BA from the University of Washington, MA from Johns Hopkins University, and PhD from the University of Michigan, Ann Arbor. Duane is a lifelong student of artists and art, including European and American Indian art, literature, and culture. For over sixty years, he's brought unique insight to his writings and publications.

Darren L. Nordlie is the 2022 first-place winner in poetry for EPIC Group Writers and has been published on the Washington State Poet Laureate's website and in *Ghost Mic Poetry* by Everett Poetry Night. He is a Hugo House scholarship recipient and served as a volunteer for a year before being promoted to vice president of the Redmond Association of Spokenword (RASP). His experiences as a biracial, neurodivergent, sensitive, well-traveled, and curious middle-aged man offer him a uniquely informed perspective. He writes poetry to wrestle with questions, self-express, and make audiences feel and/or think differently.

Victor Ortiz, Pushcart Prize nominee, has written two chapbooks—*Into Breath* and *Into Borrego Valley*—and has coauthored four multimedia books with mezzotint artist Mikio Watanabe. His work has been anthologized numerous times, and his poetry has appeared internationally in such journals as *Modern Haiku, Frogpond, Blithe Spirit, Presence, Haiku Canada Review,* and *The Mainichi.* Ortiz currently serves as a judge on the Touchstone Distinguished Books Award panel and as the Washington State Regional Coordinator for the Haiku Society of America.

Nancy Pagh burst onto the literary scene as a teenager, publishing "Is a Clam Clammy, Or Is It Just Wet?" in a local boating magazine. Tim Seibles selected her first volume, *No Sweeter Fat,* for the Autumn House Poetry Prize. She has authored three collections of poems and the creative writing guidebook *Write Moves* from Broadview Press. Nancy has been the D.H. Lawrence Fellow at the Taos Summer Writers Conference and received an Artist Trust fellowship. She teaches at Western Washington University in Bellingham. Find her at www.nancypagh.com.

Shin Yu Pai is a poet, essayist, and visual artist. She is the author of several books of poetry, including *Virga, ENSŌ, Sightings: Selected Works, AUX ARCS, Adamantine,* and *Equivalence.* She served as the fourth poet laureate of the City of Redmond from 2015 to 2017 and has been an artist-in-residence for the Seattle Art Museum and Pacific Science Center. She is a three-time fellow of MacDowell and has been in residence at Taipei Artist Village, the Ragdale Foundation, Centrum, and the National Park Service. She lives and works in the Pacific Northwest.

Charles Patterson spent his early childhood in Grand Prairie, Texas, where he used to read fly-fishing magazines tucked into his spelling book so that his parents would think he was studying. They were not fooled. He got to put his education to use during his teen years in Logan, Utah, which was in driving distance of the great trout streams of Utah, Idaho, and Wyoming. He now lives in Bellingham, where he teaches Spanish literature at Western Washington University and enjoys hiking, canoeing, and—of course—fishing with his wife, Dayna, and their two children.

Dayna Patterson is the author of *Titania in Yellow* (Porkbelly Press, 2019) and *If Mother Braids a Waterfall* (Signature Books, 2020). Honors include the Association for Mormon Letters poetry award and the 2019 #DignityNotDetention poetry prize judged by Ilya Kaminsky. Her creative work has appeared recently in *EcoTheo, Kenyon Review,* and *Whale Road Review.* She's the founding editor (now emerita) of *Psaltery & Lyre* and a coeditor of *Dove Song: Heavenly Mother in Mormon Poetry.* In her spare time, she curates Poetry + Fungus, a pairing of poetry books and species from the fungal world. daynapatterson.com.

Sylvia Byrne Pollack, a hard-of-hearing poet and retired cancer researcher, has had poems appear in *Floating Bridge Review, Crab Creek Review, The Stillwater Review,* and many others. A two-time Pushcart nominee, she won the 2013 Mason's Road Literary Award and was a 2019 Jack Straw Writer and a 2021 Mineral School resident. Her debut full-length collection, *Risking It,* was published by Red Mountain Press (2021). www.sylviabyrnepollack.com.

Cynthia R. Pratt is one of the founding members of the Olympia Poetry Network's board, which has been in existence for over thirty years. One of her poems was accepted for display at the Seattle Salmon Strategy Summit 2005. She was a biologist for the Washington Department of Fish and Wildlife before retirement. Her manuscript *Celestial Drift* was published in 2017. She was a Lacey councilmember and the deputy mayor of the City of Lacey for the last twelve years, her term ending in December 2021. She is the first poet laureate of Lacey as of 2022.

Jennifer Preston is an award-winning eco-author, poet, and artist focused on advocacy and the complex mind-body relationship. Born in Southern California and educated at UC Berkeley, she now lives in Washington, where she regularly frolics in the woods and water discovering her lost childhood. "Sharing my passion for our planet and the people on it motivates me to distill concepts and connect ideas that make our environment and bodies healthy and whole. My goal is to rekindle a sense of wonder, ignite curiosity, and be a conduit to conversation in the community." Connect at www.byjenn.com.

Laura Read is the author of *But She Is Also Jane,* forthcoming from University of Massachusetts Press in 2023, *Dresses from the Old Country* (BOA, 2018), *Instructions for My Mother's Funeral* (University of Pittsburgh Press, 2012), and *The Chewbacca on Hollywood Boulevard Reminds Me of You* (Floating Bridge Press, 2011). She served as poet laureate for Spokane from 2015 to 2017 and teaches at Spokane Falls Community College and Eastern Washington University.

Kate Reavey coordinates Studium Generale at Peninsula College and directs the Foothills Writers Series. Her chapbooks are *Through the East Window* (Sagittarius Press), *Trading Posts* (Tangram), and *Too Small to Hold You* (Pleasure Boat Studio). From 2014 to 2018, she taught in ʔaʔkʷustəŋáwtxʷ House of Learning, Peninsula College Longhouse, for the Native Pathways Program through The Evergreen State College. Her first full collection of poems, *Curve,* was published in October 2022.

Bethany Reid's *Sparrow* won the 2012 Gell Poetry Prize, selected by Dorianne Laux. Her stories, poetry, and essays have recently appeared in *One Art, Poetry East, Quartet, Passengers, Adelaide,* and *Persimmon Tree.* Bethany and her husband live in Edmonds near their grown daughters. She blogs about writing and life at http://bethanyareid.com.

Richard Revoyr: Born 1954 in Monroe, Washington. Taught grades 3–8 for thirty-three years in Washington State. Air Force veteran. Gratefully married for a hell of a long time: always. Likes to fish, hunt, water ski, and write a bit.

Susan Rich is the author of five poetry collections: *Gallery of Postcards and Maps: New and Selected Poems* (Salmon Poetry), as well as *Cloud Pharmacy, The Alchemist's Kitchen, Cures Include Travel,* and *The Cartographer's Tongue: Poems of the World* (all from White Pine Press). Her poems have received awards from the Fulbright Foundation, PEN USA, and the *Times Literary Supplement* (London). Individual poems appear in *Harvard Review, New England Review, O Magazine,* and *Witness,* among other places. Rich's sixth collection, *Blue Atlas,* is forthcoming from Red Hen Press. She is the director of Poets on the Coast: A Writing Retreat for Women.

Matthew Campbell Roberts lives in Bellingham and worked as a college writing instructor for over a decade. His first collection of poems, *A River Once More,* was recently published, and his poem "Fly Fishing Nirvana" is forthcoming in *The FlyFish Journal.* He spends time hiking Northwest trails, exploring lakes and rivers, and pursues Pacific salmon on the fly in saltwater environments.

Julie Robinett: Decided (on a whim) in late 2011 that I would memorize one poem for each week in 2012. While doing that, I fell in love with poetry. A few years later I began attending a local open mic ("just to listen")—and was soon swept into writing (and sharing) my own poetry. In addition to poetry, I love books, chocolate, shade, spiders, walking, dancing, and many kinds of music (including and especially Zimbabwean marimba music). I have lived in the Pacific Northwest for most of my life; currently my family and I (including occasional spiders) live in Everett.

Judith Roche (1941–2019) was the author of three collections of poetry: *Myrrh/My Life as a Screamer, Ghost,* and *Wisdom of the Body,* which won a 2007 American Book Award. She was coeditor of *First Fish, First People: Salmon Tales of the North Pacific Rim* and edited several poetry anthologies. She was also literary arts director emeritus for One Reel, an arts-producing company. Her work appeared in *Exquisite Corpse, Pebble Review, Wandering Hermit,* and several anthologies. She conducted poetry workshops for adults and youth in prisons and was a fellow of Black Earth Institute, the 2007 Distinguished Writer at Seattle University, and a founding member of Red Sky Poetry Theatre.

Joan Roger is a poet and physician who is fortunate to call Washington State her home. She is currently pursuing her MFA in poetry at Pacific University. Joan's poetry can be found or is forthcoming in *Thimble, Sleet, Right Hand Pointing,* and *The Healing Muse.* Joan believes in the power of poetry to transform and inspire. When she heard about Rena Priest's call for salmon poems, Joan went to her notebooks and held the salmon in her mind while reading some of her favorite poets. She gathered the lines in her cento to create a song for the salmon.

Janette Rosebrook is a lifelong resident of the Pacific Northwest, where she spent long childhood days in the woods eating salmonberries and redcaps and muddying up her good shoes in search of frogs. In 2019, she earned an MFA in creative writing from the University of British Columbia. Her current writing projects include an animated screenplay, children's books, and poetry.

April Ryan: I am a seventy-seven-year-old female; a retired twenty-seven-year Metro Seattle bus driver. My poem "Children at Play" is included on *Poems to Lean On,* and "Escape" is included on Claudia Castro Luna's *Poetic Shelters.* My work is also included on "Sharing Stories" on Northwest Prime Time (northwestprimetime.com). *April Blossoms* (2020) is available on Amazon.

Jacob D. Salzer enjoys writing haiku, senryu, tanka, and haibun and is the managing editor of four haiku anthologies: *Yanty's Butterfly: Haiku Nook: An Anthology, Half a Rainbow: Haiku Nook: An Anthology, Desert Rain: Haiku Nook: An Anthology,* and *New Bridges: A Haiku Anthology* from the Portland Haiku Group. He is the coauthor, with Michelle Hyatt, of *Echoes: A Collection of Linked-Verse Poetry.* His solo poetry collections include *Mare Liberum: Haiku & Tanka* (Lulu, 2020), inspired by water and the sea, and *Unplugged—Haiku & Tanka* (Lulu, 2022), inspired by Mother Earth and Michelle Hyatt. Jacob also edits the *Haiku Poet Interviews* blog.

Caitlin Scarano is a writer based in Bellingham. She holds a PhD from the University of Wisconsin-Milwaukee. Her second full-length collection of poems, *The Necessity of Wildfire,* was selected by Ada Limón as the winner of the Wren Poetry Prize. In May

2021, Bear Gallery (Fairbanks, Alaska) exhibited Caitlin's and Megan Perra's collaborative project *The Ten-Oh-Two*—poems and visual art on the Porcupine caribou herd. Caitlin is a member of the Washington Wolf Advisory Group. In 2018, she was selected as a participant in the National Science Foundation's Antarctic Artists & Writers Program. Find her at caitlinscarano.com.

Steve Schinnell, ah hoo boy. The hard part. Let's see. B. 1951. D. well, let's skip that for now. Timber cutter land surveyor forest engineer cabinet maker sawmiller bowl turner woodcarver itinerate scribbler voracious reader semihermitous husband and father of four daughters still clueless about girls. devoted to all things violin. live surrounded by forest, always unavailable for comment.

Carla Shafer's poems appear in *Whatcom Places II, Noisy Waters, For Love of Orcas, Last Call, Crosscurrents,* and *Clover.* She has published four chapbooks and one choral music piece, *Elixir of the Solar Spectrum.* She founded the Open Mic Chuckanut Sandstone Writers Theater in 1991 in Bellingham, where she lives. She has published *Peace Poems: Featuring International Poets from British Columbia and the Pacific Northwest* and the poetry anthologies *Our Deepest Calling* (2020) and *Solstice: Light and Dark of the Salish Sea* (2021). A graduate in English from Lewis & Clark College, Portland, Oregon, she was accepted as a 2023 Jack Straw Writer.

Katy Shedlock is a pastor and poet in the west central neighborhood of Spokane, just below the falls. Her poetry has been featured online by *Earth & Altar, Line Rider Press,* and *Pontoon Poetry* and published locally in *The Inlander.* She is currently an MFA candidate at Eastern Washington University, and before COVID, she competed in local and national poetry slams. You can find her @rev_katy or walking the Centennial Trail with her husband, Ben, and her dog, Salem.

Misty Shipman is a writer, director, producer, and poet. She holds an MFA in creative writing from the University of Idaho and is pursuing a PhD in film and literature from Washington State University. An impassioned creator, she began winning national writing awards at the age of seventeen. Early honors include the Barnes & Noble Katie Herzog Young Writer's Award, the Kay Snow Award in Adult Fiction (first place), the Grace Nixon Fellowship, the Hemingway Fellowship, and more. Misty began directing professionally in 2019.

Martha Silano is the author of five books of poetry. Her most recent collection, *Gravity Assist,* appeared from Saturnalia Books in 2019. Previous collections include *Reckless Lovely* (2014) and *The Little Office of the Immaculate Conception* (2011), also from Saturnalia Books. Martha's poems have appeared in *Poetry, Paris Review, AGNI, Poetry Daily, Kenyon Review, The American Poetry Review,* and *The Best American Poetry* series, among others. She teaches at Bellevue College.

Lauren Silver's writings appear in *The Madrona Project: Keep a Green Bough* and *The Madrona Project: Human Communities in Wild Places.* She resides in the traditional territory of the Suquamish people, the People of the Clear Salt Water, in Washington State. Her home is a precious little nest of a one-room cabin—a cabin who's a young beauty, not an old lady. Her neighbors, a mix of native trees and shrubs, inhale and exhale close by, on a ridge above the salty Salish Sea in a region whose conversations often refer to some form of this one word: water. More of her writing is on apileofsticks.wordpress.com and gracewithindementia.com.

George Silverstar was born and mostly raised on the Yakama Reservation in eastern Washington. His poetry and prolific letters reveal the passion of a man plagued by mental illness and a deep conflict with his Native American heritage, who ultimately took his own life but left a wake of beauty and art behind him. His poems explore concepts of nature, conflict, lost love, and the joy of being a father. A book of his collected poems, *Silverstar,* was published in 1992 by Sagittarius Press, Port Townsend.

Suzanne Simons is a professor at The Evergreen State College in Olympia, where she teaches poetry and community studies. She helped establish the City of Olympia's poet laureate position and is a member of the Olympia Poetry Network. She has taught poetry at the Washington Corrections Center and other community-based workshops. Her work has appeared in the journals *Cirque, Aethlon: The Journal of Sports Literature,* and *Western Friend,* in stone at a skate park, and in a photography/poetry exhibit at the Josephy Center for Arts and Culture in Joseph, Oregon. She enjoys watching salmon spawn each fall in McLane Creek.

Sheila Sondik, printmaker and poet, lives in Bellingham, where she is awed by the sight of salmon fighting their way up a roaring waterfall to reach their natal waters. She was born in Hartford, Connecticut, graduated from Harvard College, and then moved to the West Coast, where the landscape felt like home to her. A poet and visual artist since childhood, she began writing Japanese forms of poetry in 2010 and has studied other Asian arts, including ikebana and Chinese calligraphy. The Northwest landscape and its denizens are a constant inspiration. Her poetry has been widely published. www.sheilasondik.com.

Ann Spiers served as Vashon Island's inaugural poet laureate and stewards its Poetry Post in the town center. Her 2021–22 publications include *Rain Violent* (Empty Bowl), *Back Cut* (Black Heron), and *Harpoon* (Ravenna's Triple Series #16). She actively supports the island's Audubon chapter, land trust, parks department, and the Vashon Nature Center in conserving the island's ecosystems that host salmon. Vashon is the traditional lands and waters of the sxʷəbabs (Schwa ba sh), the island's native people. See annspiers.com.

Joannie Stangeland is the author of several poetry collections, most recently *The Scene You See.* She has received the *Crosswinds Poetry Journal*'s grand prize and the Floating Bridge Press chapbook award. Her poems have also appeared in *Two Hawks Quarterly, SWWIM, Prairie Schooner, New England Review,* and other journals. Joannie holds an MFA from the Rainier Writing Workshop.

Scott T. Starbuck taught ecopoetry workshops the past three years at Scripps Institution of Oceanography in the Master of Advanced Studies Program in Climate Science and Policy program at UC San Diego. His book of climate poems, *Hawk on Wire,* was a July 2017 Editor's Pick at NewPages.com and selected from more than 1,500 books as a 2018 Montaigne Medal finalist at the Eric Hoffer Awards for "the most thought-provoking books." Starbuck's *Trees, Fish, and Dreams Climateblog* at riverseek.blogspot.com has over 100,000 views from readers in 110 countries. *Between River & Street* (MoonPath Press, 2021) documents Pacific Northwest salmon culture before it may be gone.

Sarah Stockton is the founder/editor of *River Mouth Review.* She is also the author of two poetry chapbooks: *Time's Apprentice* (dancing girl press, 2021) and *Castaway* (Glass Lyre Press, 2022). More published poems can be found at www.sarahstockton.com. Sarah lives in Port Townsend.

Ed Stover is a retired daily newspaper journalist who lives in Yakima. He is active in the Yakima Coffeehouse Poets community.

John Streamas is an associate professor of ethnic studies and American studies at Washington State University in Pullman. I am also a graduate of Syracuse's writing program, where my advisors were George P. Elliott and Raymond Carver. My publications include several critical essays in journals and collections as well as stories and poems, including three poems forthcoming in *The Asian American Literary Review.* As a Japanese American born in Japan, I have an interest in Asian American history and culture and am writing a book on the Bomb, alternative temporalities, and race.

Poet and painter **Robert Sund** (1929–2001) grew up on a small farm in Washington's Chehalis Valley, studied with poet Theodore Roethke at the University of Washington, and lived most of his life in Washington's rural Skagit Valley. He was a fisherman in Southeast Alaska and worked the wheat harvests of eastern Washington. His poetry reflects a deep lifelong engagement with landscape and community. He is author of *Poems from Ish River Country: Collected Poetry and Translations* and *Notes from Disappearing Lake: The River Journals of Robert Sund,* among other titles. His work is available through the Robert Sund Poet's House, www.robertsund.org.

Rick Swann lives in Seattle. He is a retired elementary school librarian and a member of the Greenwood Poets. His children's book, *Our School Garden!,* a series of linked poems about how a community can grow from a garden, was awarded the Growing Good Kids Book Award from the American Horticultural Society.

Madeline Sweet is a student at Western Washington University and is currently studying environmental science. I would eventually like to study hydrology. Science uses math and numbers to tell stories and that is what I hope to do—tell stories both through data analysis and life.

Mary Ellen Talley's poems have been published in over one hundred journals and anthologies. Her poems have received three Pushcart nominations. Her chapbook *Postcards from the Lilac City* was published by Finishing Line Press in 2020. Born and raised in Washington, she earned an MSPA at the University of Washington, after which she spent four decades serving students with communication disabilities in Federal Way and Seattle public schools as a speech-language pathologist. Her reviews of poetry collections appear widely.

Matteo Tamburini is, in order, / a father, husband, and a limerician. / He grew up far from here, across the water, / professionally he's a mathematician. / An honor for the simple words he authored / to be in this felicitous collection. / His catchphrase is that "math is all around us" / and hopes together we'll seek peace and justice.

Joanna Thomas is a poet and visual artist residing in the small university town of Ellensburg. She is the author of the chapbook *blue•bird (bloo–burd)* from Milk & Cake Press (2021) and the limited-edition artist chapbooks *rabbit: an erasure poem* (2018) and *cuddle fluttering my feather heart* (2018). Her poems have appeared in the journals *Picture Sentence, Found Poetry Review,* and *Petrichor* as well as several anthologies, including *WA 129.* Her work has been supported with grants from Washington State Artist Trust, Allied Arts Foundation, and Ellensburg City Arts Commission.

Earle Thompson's work has been included in many anthologies, including *Harper's Anthology of 20th Century Native American Poets* (Harper & Row), *Anthology of Third World Writing* (Pig Iron Press), and *Songs of This Earth on Turtle's Back* (Greenfield Review Press). He has also published work in *Akewon, AtlAtl, Argus, Blue Cloud Quarterly, Contact II, Greenfield Review, Northwest Arts, Northwest Indian News, Portland Review, Prison Writing Review, Wicazo Sa Review,* and others. His collection of poetry, *The Juniper Moon Pulls at My Bones,* was published in 1985 by Blue Cloud Quarterly Press and won the Written Arts competition in the annual Bumbershoot Literary Arts festival in Seattle.

Kathleen Tice started writing haiku in the mid-1980s while helping with the publication of *Dragonfly East/West Haiku Quarterly.*

Richard Tice began writing haiku in 1976 while teaching English in Japan. His haiku first appeared in *Bonsai* and *Modern Haiku* in 1978. In 1985 he assumed editorship of *Dragonfly,* adding translations of contemporary Japanese haiku and publishing sixteen issues. His book *Station Stop* was awarded second prize in the 1985–86 Haiku Society of America Merit Books Award. His second poetry book, *Familiar & Foreign: Haiku and Linked Verse,* was issued in 2008 from Waking Lion Press. Richard has published numerous articles on Japanese haiku and haikai and translated several hundred Japanese haiku.

Tito Titus, author of *I can still smile like Errol Flynn* (Empty Bowl Press, 2015), appeared in 2020 with Garrison Keillor to present two of Tito's death poems on Keillor's *The Writer's Almanac.* Tito's poetry and satire have appeared in *Puget Soundings, Argus, Seattle Post-Intelligencer, Red Light District: Seattle Erotic Art Festival's Literary Art Anthology* (Foundation for Sex Positive Culture, 2011), *Poets Unite! LitFUSE 10th Anniversary Anthology* (Cave Moon Press, 2016), Paco-Michelle Atwood's *World Inside Designer Jeans* (AuthorHouse, 2013), *The Little Red Anthology* (Little Red Press, 2009), *Pandemic Poetry* (Headline Poetry & Press, 2020), and *In Parentheses Journal* (2020).

Gail Tremblay is a descendant of Onondaga and Micmac ancestors. She resides in Olympia and has been an artist, writer, and cultural critic for over thirty years. Her book of poems *Indian Singing* was published by CALYX Press, and her book of poems *Farther from and Too Close to Home* was published by Lone Willow Press. Her poetry is widely anthologized, and poems have been translated into French, German, Spanish, and Japanese and published internationally.

Arianne True (Choctaw, Chickasaw) is a queer poet and folk artist from Seattle. She teaches and mentors young poets around Puget Sound and moonlights as a copyeditor. Arianne has received fellowships from Jack Straw, Hugo House, and Artist Trust, and is a proud alum of Hedgebrook and of the MFA program at the Institute of American Indian Arts. She was recently the Seattle Repertory Theater's first Native artist-in-residence.

Kathryn True is a poet and writer inspired by the Salish Sea. A lifelong Northwesterner, for the past twenty-two years she has made her home on Vashon Island near Seattle. Kathryn volunteers with Vashon Nature Center, where she gives voice to water bears, bird's nest fungi, and brown creepers to connect people with nature. She deepens her own relationship with the natural world through haiku, poems, and prose that celebrate and mourn ecosystems facing uncertain futures. Kathryn is coauthor of *Nature in the City: Seattle,* and her poems appear in *Kingfisher Journal, Worth More Standing,* and *Mondays at Three: Portage.*

Cindy Veach's most recent book, *Her Kind* (CavanKerry Press), was named a finalist for the 2022 Eric Hoffer Montaigne Medal. She is also the author of *Gloved Against Blood* (CavanKerry Press), a finalist for the Paterson Poetry Prize and a Massachusetts Center for the Book Must Read, and the chapbook *Innocents* (Nixes Mate). Her poems have appeared in the Academy of American Poets Poem-a-Day, *AGNI, Michigan Quarterly Review, Poet Lore, The Journal,* and *Salamander,* among others. She is the recipient of the Philip Booth Poetry Prize and the Samuel Allen Washington Prize. Cindy is poetry coeditor of *Mom Egg Review* (MER). www.cindyveach.com.

Julene Tripp Weaver is a psychotherapist and writer in Seattle. Her third collection, *truth be bold: Serenading Life & Death in the Age of AIDS,* was a finalist for the Lambda Literary Awards and won the Bisexual Book Award. Her book *No Father Can Save Her* is now also available as an e-book. Her work is published in many journals and anthologies, a few of which are *Verse-Virtual, The Seattle Review of Books, HIV Here & Now, Mad Swirl, Journal of the Plague Years, Global Poemic, MookyChick,* and the anthology *Poets Speaking to Poets: Echoes and Tributes.*

Michael Dylan Welch served two terms as Redmond poet laureate. He's also president of the Redmond Association of Spokenword and curates SoulFood Poetry Night. He's a former vice president of the Haiku Society of America, cofounder and director of Haiku North America and the Seabeck Haiku Getaway, cofounder of the American Haiku Archives, and founder and president of the Tanka Society of America. He also runs National Haiku Writing Month (www.nahaiwrimo.com). His website, devoted mostly to haiku, is www.graceguts.com. Michael has published dozens of books, mostly haiku, and lives in Sammamish, with his wife and two teenagers.

Travis Wellman is the operations manager of the Stonerose Interpretive Center and Eocene Fossil Site, where he plays with fifty-million-year-old fossils. After working with thousands of fossils over the years, he has been captivated the most by one particular specimen from there—*Eosalmo driftwoodensis,* an extinct salmonid ancestor to salmon and trout. Though not migratory like some of its modern descendants, *Eosalmo* journeyed through the eons to instigate his interests in paleontology.

Jonathan Went is a teacher, poet, and writer. His work focuses on the spiritual connection between humans and nature. He has been published in *LitMagazine* and has work forthcoming in *Listen,* published by Spiritual Directors International. He has been shortlisted for the Pangaea Prize and also the Geminga Poetry Prize. He is a member of The Well in Seattle, where he lives.

Thena Westfall has been a registered nurse for over a decade in Port Angeles. She has been writing poetry for even longer than that. She is a third-generation resident of

Clallam County determined to continue the cultivation of skills, conservation, and understanding for the land she grew up in.

In large part for the salmon, **Leslie Wharton** moved to Bellingham after losing her home in a Colorado wildfire. She and her partner built that off-grid solar home with their own hands. Survival instincts triggered their desire to live where salmon, berries, and rain are plentiful. Fishing, being by the sea or rivers, calms her. Compassion, the positive outcome of trauma, led her to become a caregiver for the elderly and a poet.

Griffith H. Williams, owner and operator of East Point West Press, has been a fixture of the Pacific Northwest poetry scene for years. Since 1991, he has used an antique letterpress to produce annual chapbooks of poetry for himself and others. Formally trained in the poetic techniques of a Welsh bard, many of his works appear under his bardic name Gruffydd Hirwallt.

Wren Winfield moved from Santa Fe, New Mexico, to Chimacum, Washington, in August 2020 to be closer to her aging father. The Olympic Peninsula inspires Wren's poetry, song lyrics, and short films. Wren received her BA in creative writing from UC Santa Cruz in 1984 and attended graduate school at San Francisco State in filmmaking. Wren's father, **Richard Starkey Seaman,** was born in New York in 1929. Richard moved from Boston to Port Angeles in 2002, after retiring from his career as a counseling psychologist. Richard now enjoys collaborating on poems with his daughter Wren.

Bill Yake, a poet/naturalist/scientist, lived with his wife, Jeannette, overlooking Green Cove Creek—a chum salmon stream running to the southern end of the Salish Sea. His poems appear widely in anthologies and publications serving environmental and literary communities. These include *Open Spaces, Orion, Rattle, Cascadia Review,* and NPR's *Krulwich's Wonders.* Bill's poetry collections include *This Old Riddle: Cormorants and Rain; Unfurl, Kite, and Veer* (both from Radiolarian Press); and, most recently, a collection of new and selected poems, *Waymaking by Moonlight* (Empty Bowl Press). Bill Yake passed away in December 2022.

Maya Jewell Zeller is the author of the interdisciplinary collaboration (with visual artist Carrie DeBacker) *Alchemy for Cells & Other Beasts,* the chapbook *Yesterday, the Bees,* and the poetry collection *Rust Fish;* her humor writing appears in such places as *Booth* and *Necessary Fiction.* Recipient of a Promise Award from the Sustainable Arts Foundation as well as a residency in the H.J. Andrews Experimental Forest, Maya is an associate professor of English for Central Washington University and affiliate poetry faculty for Western Colorado University's low-residency MFA. Find Maya on Twitter @MayaJZeller.

Empty Bowl Press is located on land that is the traditional and contemporary territory of the S'Klallam (Nəxʷsʎ́áyəm) and the Chemakum (Aqokúlo or Čə́məqə̓m) peoples. We are grateful for their ongoing stewardship of this land and are committed to continued education and action that upholds and honors the Indigenous experience, past and present.

Poems are set in Adobe Caslon Pro, with titles in Century Gothic.
Printed on archival paper.

www.emptybowl.org